pie

pie

pie

pie

by John Phillip Carroll

photographs by Tina Rupp

pie pie
pie
easy homemade favorites
pie

CHRONICLE BOOKS
SAN FRANCISCO

Text copyright © 2005 by John Phillip Carroll.

Photographs copyright © 2005 by Tina Rupp.

All rights reserved. No part of this book may be reproduced in any form without written permission from the publisher.

Library of Congress Cataloging-in-Publication Data available.

ISBN 978-0-8118-3930-3

Manufactured in Singapore.

Designed by Leon Yu
Photo Assistance by Teresa Horgan
Prop styling by Stephanie Basralian
Food styling by Alison Attenborough

10 9 8 7 6 5 4

Chronicle Books LLC
680 Second Street
San Francisco, California 94107

www.chroniclebooks.com

This book is dedicated to Marion Cunningham, my chief pie inspiration.

table of contents

introduction

More than almost any other dessert, pie for me has stood for what is good and nurturing about American life. If an array of sweets is offered, at a potluck for example, I'm apt to head for the pie. Sometimes I am disappointed, but seeing a pie, or group of pies, on a table always makes me feel optimistic.

When I ask people what their favorite dessert is, most, particularly those over forty, answer "Pie." This is usually followed by a wistful story about meals at home, followed by a lament about their own lack of pie-making talent and the fact that they haven't had a really good pie in years. Unfortunately, the simple skills for making pies with wonderful taste and texture seem to have been almost lost and are all too often associated with an elderly grandmother, aunt, or neighbor from the past.

In perusing much of what has been written about pies in the last decade or so, I'm struck by how often pie baking is transformed into something quite time-consuming, even intimidating. What was once an elementary technique, learned in home economics or by watching someone in the kitchen, has been made frightening. I know many good cooks who are comfortable tackling duck confit, or veal Orloff, yet feel completely inept when faced with the few simple ingredients that go into a pie crust. The same view pertains to the blending of a basic salad dressing, judging from the supermarket shelf space given to bottled dressings. While pie crust and dressing might not seem related, they are similar in that, with the right balance and handling of three or four modest ingredients, you will have success, with results that taste better than anything you can buy, for a fraction of the price.

I imagine the first person to say that something was "easy as pie" did it for a reason, and I suspect he or she didn't find pie baking as daunting as it is perceived to be today. In this book, I will try to unlock, or to explain, what it is that gives pies a difficult reputation, and then remove the fear with clear information for success. This is the kind of advice you would get from having a patient, knowledgeable friend look over your shoulder.

To beginning bakers I say, forget what scares you about making pies, and start fresh. Just forge ahead and remember that a good pie doesn't have to be cosmetically perfect—that's part of the charm and appeal of home baking. Instant success might be rare, but it is also rare in making pancakes or muffins, or in public speaking, or in learning how to ride a bicycle or drive a car. It's practice that helps you develop a natural feel for anything.

A good pie is a triumph, based on a crisp and flaky crust and a tender filling that has just enough texture to hold together when cut. While a batch of cookies might stay fresh and crisp for several days, most pies do not keep well, and are best fresh. A short shelf life can be a pie's downfall. That's why pies turned out in the automated world, where they are built to last, are so often disappointing.

One of the best bakers I know, Marion Cunningham, recalls her early pie-making days in the 1940s, when she was learning to cook and bake by asking neighbors what they cooked: "If the pies weren't good, we didn't know it. We didn't think like that then We didn't dissect things then, nobody's palate was jaded, nor was anyone a critic. I've always felt, you can eat it even if it doesn't turn out; it's always worth tasting."

I can't think of any sounder, more assuring words. So don't agonize over your pies, and don't be afraid of them. Pie baking is generally forgiving, and you don't need to have the precision of a chemist to be good at it.

pie basics

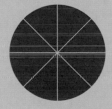

equipment

Your senses, your ability to touch, to smell, and to see, are among your best assets in pie baking. That's why I urge you to make dough by hand, so you know how it feels when it's just right. Similarly, open the oven door and take a quick glance at a pie as it bakes, and notice how it looks and smells, so you can remember the toasty aroma of a fully baked crust, or the aroma of sweet, bubbling juices. When you are comfortable making pies, your own good judgment is often a better gauge than time and temperature.

Pastry Blender

When I make a pie crust, I like to get my hands right into the shortening and flour and blend them together with my fingers. If you are uncomfortable doing that, a pastry blender will also do the job. This hand-held tool is made of parallel strands of horseshoe-shaped wires, anchored on both ends by a wooden or plastic handle. By repeatedly plunging the pastry blender into the ingredients as you move it about and rotate the bowl, you use the wires, rather than your fingers, to blend the shortening into the flour.

Rolling Pin

For rolling out pie dough, a rolling pin is almost essential, but you don't need to spend a mint to get one that's right for the job. I have several, and my favorite is a 20-inch-long piece of ordinary wooden doweling, about 1¼ inches in diameter, available at any lumberyard or hardware store. If you want a pin with handles, a wooden one with a roller about 10 inches long (that's not including the handles) will do the job. If you opt for a large, heavy, professional-size pin (up to 30 inches long and weighing 4 to 5 pounds), with or without handles, be sure your work area allows you ample room to maneuver, because you'll need a generous space to handle such a pin.

Pie Pans

Pie pans are alternately known as pie plates and pie dishes. My assortment, like my rolling pin collection, is large. My favorites are clear glass (Pyrex) pans. They measure 9 inches across—that's from inside rim to inside rim—and 1¼ inches deep, with a liquid capacity of 4 cups. Prebaked pie shells and filled crusts brown nicely in them. In fact, I have found glass pans to be good insurance against a soggy bottom crust—not a perfect answer, but the easiest solution. Glass is also a snap to clean. Each recipe in this book was prepared in such a pan.

Sturdy metal pans with a shiny aluminum or brushed silver surface bake well enough, and they are indestructible, but crusts don't brown quite as well in them. Disposable aluminum pans are passable, especially if you have lots of pies to make for a party, but you should stack two of them together: They are flimsy otherwise and can buckle when you move a filled pie, and a sharp knife can also slice right through the pan when cutting.

Whichever type of pan you use, the diameter and capacity can vary from manufacturer to manufacturer, regardless of what the label says. To be certain, get out a ruler and a measuring cup, and gauge both for yourself.

Rolling Surface

The surface on which you roll out pie dough can be just about anything, as long as it is smooth, flat, clean, and cool. I use a large wooden board or an acrylic cutting slab. Formica and granite countertops are also good work surfaces. A polished marble slab is dandy for all kinds of pastry work, but is awfully weighty and expensive if you are baking pies only occasionally.

Wire Whisks

I find whisks essential, both for stirring together dry ingredients in the most thorough way without sifting, and for the smoothest blending of cream and custard fillings, in either a mixing bowl or a saucepan. One or two whisks, about 12 inches long and with a network of looped wires 2 to 2½ inches wide, are plenty for your pie-making needs.

Some cooks are comfortable using a massive hand-held "balloon" whisk and a substantial amount of their own elbow grease for whipping several egg whites for chiffon fillings and meringue toppings. But I consider that too much work and prefer to depend on electricity.

Beaters

A heavy-duty stand-type electric mixer is rarely essential in pie making, but it is extremely useful for mixing up cookie and bread doughs and cake batters. A heavy, powerful machine with a dough hook, paddle, and whip attachments and a deep, rounded bowl will likely carry a hefty price tag, but it will give you a lifetime of service in return.

A portable hand-held electric mixer is a godsend for whipping large amounts of cream and beating egg whites for meringue. It works anywhere there's an outlet, and you can stick it in a drawer when you are done, so it doesn't take up any counter space. It is well worth the reasonable cost, but look around and ask friends what they use, because a higher price does not always indicate a better mixer.

A hand-held rotary beater, known more nostalgically as an eggbeater or a Dover beater, is indispensable for whipping up a small amount of cream or a couple of eggs or egg whites, especially if you don't have a hand-held electric mixer.

Measuring Cups

Dry ingredients, particularly flour, should be measured evenly and consistently. For that, it's helpful to have a graduated, stacked set of "dry" measuring cups, in ¼-, ⅓-, ½-, and 1-cup sizes. They should have straight sides and level tops, and it doesn't matter whether they are made of plastic or metal. As I describe later in the section on flour, you can "scoop and level" these cups for even measurements.

Liquids are easier to measure in cups with graduated markings on the side and a spout for nondribble pouring. Get glass or translucent plastic so you can read the cups from the outside, at eye level. You'll find the 1- and 2-cup sizes especially useful. A 4-cup measure is not only good for measuring, but its deep, straight sides also make it the perfect container for whipping cream with a minimum of splattering. Glass cups are handy for microwave use, such as melting butter and chocolate. I don't recommend using plastic cups in the microwave.

Measuring Spoons

You should have at least one set of graduated measuring spoons, of either metal or plastic, for measuring small amounts of dry ingredients like salt and spices. The capacity of measuring spoons (and occasionally of measuring cups) varies by manufacturer, regardless of the ¼-teaspoon, ½-teaspoon, 1-teaspoon, and 1-tablespoon markings. In baking, consistent measurements using the same utensils are probably more important than absolute accuracy. Whatever spoons and cups you use, use the same ones all the time.

Ovens

Keep in mind that ovens, like people, have idiosyncrasies. No two are exactly alike, and each distributes heat differently. Therefore, you should get to know your oven and keep mental—or actual—notes on how it behaves. Do you find "hot spots," where things brown well, and "cool spots," where they brown hardly at all? For most home baking, such quirks aren't a problem, as long as you know about them and make adjustments in rack placement or rotation during baking.

ingredients

Complexity is not a quality I associate with pie-making ingredients. They are simple and widely available. Therefore, I don't recommend substituting one ingredient for another, because it can make a difference—and often not a favorable one—in the results.

Flour

With one exception, these recipes use all-purpose flour. It works well for pie crusts and for thickening some pie fillings, and it does not need to be sifted. There is no noticeable flavor or texture difference between a pie crust made with bleached flour and one made with unbleached flour, and you may use either one. To measure flour, plunge a level, dry measuring cup into the flour container, scoop up a heaping cup of flour, and then sweep off the excess with a table knife, to make an even measure.

Sugars

Unless I indicate otherwise, whenever a recipe calls for sugar, I'm referring to granulated white sugar. Don't replace it with honey or other sweeteners, because they react differently with other ingredients, and there is no sound rule of thumb for their substitution. You can't always switch them measure for measure with good results.

To measure brown sugar, pack it into a cup, pressing it down with your fingers or the back of a spoon. It should hold its shape when turned out. Light brown sugar and dark brown sugar are quite interchangeable in these recipes, although dark brown sugar has a more pronounced flavor.

Vegetable Shortening

Conventional shortening is made of vegetable oil that has been hydrogenated, so it is solid at room temperature, and almost flavorless. Though it adds little taste of its own, this is the fat I prefer for making a flaky, crisp, tender American pie crust. (Adding fat to make crust flaky and tender is, in time-honored terms, "shortening" it.) It keeps indefinitely without refrigeration, and its soft consistency makes it easy to blend into flour. It is generally very forgiving of rerolling or a little too much handling—a particular plus if you are new to pie making.

There is also a trans-fat-free shortening available at this writing. It is made of palm oil, a highly saturated fat that is naturally solid at room temperature, without hydrogenation. It has a slightly more pronounced flavor than conventional shortening, and I find it makes a crust that is firmer and less tender. In a side-by-side comparison, a vegetable shortening crust was the hands-down winner, trans fats and all.

To measure vegetable shortening, pack it into a measuring cup, pressing it down with your fingers or a rubber spatula to the level you want. Use your fingers or the spatula to scoop it out of the cup.

Eggs

The recipes in this book use graded "large" eggs. Some recipes call for the eggs to be separated. This does not mean moving them away from the other ingredients or from one another. It is the technique of liberating the white from the yolk, an essential step in making meringues, as well as cream and chiffon pie fillings. Eggs will separate more easily if they are chilled, and the best method is the most tactile. Crack the shell by giving it a couple of sharp knocks against the rim of a bowl, then open the eggshell and let the egg slide into the slightly cupped fingers of one hand held over the bowl. Jiggle your hand a little and gently slide the egg about, letting the white fall between your fingers and into the bowl. Drop the yolk into another bowl. If you get any yolk in the whites, simply scoop it out with a piece of shell. It does not matter whether egg whites are chilled or at room temperature when you beat them; the volume is the same either way.

Sometimes a recipe does call for eggs to be at room temperature. This is because they will blend more smoothly into the other ingredients than chilled eggs. To bring refrigerator-cold eggs rapidly to room temperature, put them (uncracked and in their shells) into a bowl and cover them with hot tap water for a couple of minutes to take the chill off.

Dried Fruit

Dried fruit used in pies should be moist and a little chewy, and it should taste like the fruit itself. (I include dates in this assessment, although they are not actually dried.) If you have dried fruit that has been in the cupboard for a long time, and you find it's gotten hard and granular, you can soften it by covering it with boiling water and letting it sit for 10 minutes. Drain it thoroughly, then taste it. If it's tired and stale tasting, don't use it.

pie crusts

If you are going to learn to cook, pie crust is a good addition to your reper-
toire. And once you learn, you will wonder why people find it so intimidating.
There are a couple of ways to go about making pie crust, and you need to
master only one of them. If the results aren't perfect right off the bat—
if your crust is a little tough or rustic looking—console yourself with the
knowledge that it will probably be better next time. The goodness of a
homemade pie is in its flavor, not how it looks.

I like traditional pie crusts, so here you will find a Basic All-American Pie
Dough and a Boiling Water Pie Dough, suitable for any pie, along with a
couple of flavored doughs, including one made with chocolate and nuts
and another with cornmeal, for times when you want to branch out and be
more adventurous. Each of these recipes makes a generous amount of
dough, since it is far easier to work with too much than too little, and you
can use any trimmings for patching tears and holes.

Homemade pie dough will keep, patted into a disk shape and wrapped
snugly in plastic wrap, for two to three days in the refrigerator. After that
its freshly made taste begins to fade. Dough made with unbleached flour

will also begin to turn gray. Let dough that is thoroughly chilled sit at room temperature for about an hour before rolling it out. Microwaving it for a few seconds to bring it quickly to room temperature is not a good idea.

Unbaked pie dough can be frozen for up to three months. Wrap it tightly in plastic, then slip it into a plastic bag, press out the air, and seal the bag. A tight seal and an air-free environment are keys to keeping good flavor and color intact. To use the dough, thaw it overnight in the refrigerator, then let it sit at room temperature for an hour or so before rolling it out.

Although I prefer to refrigerate or freeze dough before I roll it out, the same guidelines apply to storing unbaked pie shells: Place the rolled-out dough, in its pie pan, inside a large plastic bag. Press out as much air as possible and seal the bag, then place it inside another bag and seal tightly. If you have frozen dough in a glass pan, let it come to room temperature before putting it in a hot oven.

Store-bought refrigerated, frozen, and packaged crusts are okay to fall back on in a pinch, but I have tried them all and have often been disappointed, because they lack the fresh flavor and texture of a homemade crust.

basic all-american pie dough

Crisp and flaky, this dough is suitable for any pie. Your hands are the best tools for making it, so I urge you to plunge them right into the flour and shortening and forge ahead. You'll become familiar with the feel of the dough right away, and you'll be surprised how quick and easy it is. When friends taste your pies, they will want you to show them how you did it.

Overblending the fat and flour and adding too little water can make a crust hard rather than flaky, and mixing by hand gives you the best control. That's why I don't like to make pie dough in a food processor or mixer.

FOR A 9-INCH PIE SHELL

1½ cups all-purpose flour

½ teaspoon salt

½ cup vegetable shortening

3 to 4 tablespoons cold water

FOR A 9-INCH TWO-CRUST PIE

3 cups all-purpose flour

1 teaspoon salt

1 cup vegetable shortening

7 to 8 tablespoons cold water

Makes one 9-inch pie shell or two-crust pie

Blending the Flour and Shortening

Put the flour and salt in a large bowl—large enough to hold the ingredients, with room for your hands—and stir them together with your fingers. Drop in the shortening, and then, with your fingers, break it into several pieces as you push it around the flour. Now put both hands in the bowl, right into the flour and shortening, and rub the fingers of each hand against the thumbs, lightly blending the shortening and flour together into smaller lumps and flake-shaped pieces. Your goal is to rub the shortening into the flour while keeping the mixture light-textured and dry. Work as quickly and comfortably as you can, lifting your hands often and letting the mixture fall back into the bowl. You know you've blended enough when you don't see any lumps of shortening and you have a mixture of particles the size of coarse and fine bread crumbs.

Adding the Water

Sprinkle 1 tablespoon of water over the dough and stir briskly with a fork. Continue adding water, 1 tablespoon at a time, stirring after each addition and concentrating on the areas of the dough that seem the driest. When the dough forms a rough, cohesive mass, reach into the bowl and press the dough together into a roundish ball. If it doesn't hold together, or if parts of it seem crumbly and dry, sprinkle on a little more water. The amount of water can vary slightly from time to time, depending on your ingredients. If you are in doubt, it is better to add a little too much than not enough, because a dough that is too dry can be difficult to roll out.

Rolling Out the Dough

Have a handful of additional flour nearby in a small cup, for flouring your hands and the rolling surfaces. Rub some flour on your hands and pat the dough into a smooth cake about 1 inch thick and 3 to 4 inches across. (If you are making a two-crust pie, pat it into 2 cakes, one slightly larger than the other.)

Sprinkle your rolling surface lightly with flour, spreading the flour to cover an area about 12 inches in diameter. Put the dough in the center, using the larger piece if it is a two-crust pie, and sprinkle it lightly with flour. Flatten the dough a little with your hands, then begin rolling it into a circle. Do most of the rolling from the center out to the edges of the dough, lifting and turning it slightly every 5 or 6 rolls to help keep it round. If it sticks on the bottom, slide a long metal spatula underneath to loosen it, tossing some more flour under the dough as you lift it gently with the spatula. If the top of the dough is damp and sticky, dust it with additional flour as well. Don't be afraid to touch the dough and to use enough flour to keep it from sticking; it is really quite durable. If it tears, simply push it back together.

Although the edges will probably look uneven, keep the shape as round as possible without agonizing over it. When you have a circle 11 to 12 inches across and about 2 inches larger than the top of your pie pan, you have rolled enough.

Putting the Dough in the Pie Pan

If you are confident, you can probably just pick up the whole circle of dough and set it in the pie pan. Otherwise, try this: Roll the dough up onto the rolling pin, like a carpet. Then put the edge of the dough at the edge of the pan and unroll it, letting it drop into

the pan. If it isn't relatively centered, slide it gently so it is. If it tears, push it back together. Pat the dough snugly into the pan, starting around the edges and easing toward the center. You should have ½ to 1 inch of overhanging dough all around the pan. In places where there is more than an inch, cut it off with scissors or a sharp knife. In spots where there is less, brush the edge lightly with water and press one of the scraps of trimmed dough onto it.

If you are making a two-crust fruit pie, roll out the second piece of dough just as you did the first. Transfer it, either by lifting it or rolling it onto the rolling pin, to a sheet of waxed paper, and set it aside. Then follow the instructions given later, for a two-crust pie.

Cream, custard, and chiffon pies have only a bottom crust, called a pie shell. Depending on the recipe, the shell is filled either unbaked or fully baked.

For an Unbaked Pie Shell

Fold the overhanging dough over itself and pinch it together to make a double-thick, upstanding rim all around. Pinch the rim to make a scalloped edge—this is called fluting or crimping, and the more you do it, the easier it will become and the better you will be at it. Fill the shell and bake as directed in the recipe.

For a Fully Baked Pie Shell

Preheat the oven to 425°F. Fold and flute the rim as directed in the instructions for an unbaked pie shell, and then prick the dough all over the bottom and sides with a table fork. This should be a rapid motion, and I usually prick it 100 to 120 times. These tiny holes keep the dough from puffing up in the oven, and it is better to have too many than too few.

So the dough will hold its shape, press a 12-inch square of heavy-duty foil (or a double-thick square of regular foil) snugly into the pie shell, over the bottom and sides of the dough. Bake for about 8 minutes, until the edges of the dough are beginning to look dry but not browned. If they still look wet, bake the shell a couple minutes longer. Remove the foil and bake for 6 to 10 minutes more. Check a few minutes after you remove the foil, and if the dough is puffed in the center, prick it with a fork and it will deflate. The pie shell is done when the dough is light brown and looks dry all over. It is fragile now but will become crisp as it cools. It doesn't matter if it has shrunk a tiny bit. Set the baked pie shell aside to cool completely, and then fill it as directed in the recipe.

For a Two-Crust Pie

Put the filling into the dough-lined pan as directed in the recipe. Using your fingers, a small brush, or a wet paper towel, brush the rim of the dough generously with water. Transfer the rolled-out top crust from the waxed paper—either lift it gently or roll it onto the rolling pin—and place it over the filled pie. Press firmly all around to seal the top and bottom crusts together. Trim the edges, using a sharp knife or scissors, so you have about half an inch of overhang. Fold the overhang under itself to make a thick, upstanding rim. Flute the rim as directed in the instructions for an unbaked pie shell. With the point of a sharp knife, cut 10 to 12 slits, or vents, in the top crust, so steam can evaporate as the pie bakes. Be as random as you want with the vents, making about half of them around the edge and the rest around the center.

Two-crust fruit pies are usually baked at a high temperature for the first 15 to 20 minutes, to help brown the crust and begin cooking the filling, and then the oven is turned to a lower temperature for the remainder of the baking.

Fruit pies with juicy fillings sometimes boil over in the oven. To keep your oven clean, and to prevent a smoky kitchen, place a large sheet of heavy-duty foil on the rack under the pie to catch drips. It might not be needed, but if it is you'll be glad it's there.

It is okay to open the oven and check your pie a few times during baking. If you see the edges of the crust becoming too brown, remove the pie from the oven. Gently cover the edges with 2-inch strips of foil, bending them to fit the pie, and then return to the oven.

cornmeal pie dough

Straw colored, with a slightly sandy texture from the addition of cornmeal, this dough is compatible with any lemon, pumpkin, walnut, or pecan pie filling. This recipe makes a 9-inch pie shell; double the ingredients if you want to use it for a 9-inch two-crust pie. See the Basic All-American Pie Dough recipe (page 20) for detailed instructions on rolling out and using the dough.

1 cup all-purpose flour

½ cup yellow cornmeal

½ teaspoon salt

½ cup vegetable shortening

3 to 4 tablespoons cold water

Makes one 9-inch pie shell

In a medium bowl, combine the flour, cornmeal, and salt and stir them together with a fork or whisk until evenly mixed. Add the shortening and, using your fingertips or a pastry blender, work it into the dry ingredients until the mixture looks like coarse, fresh bread crumbs. Add the water, 1 tablespoon at a time, stirring with a fork after each addition. This dough tends to be quite soft, so add just enough water for it to hold together in a rough, damp mass; you might not need the full amount.

Flour your hands and pat the dough into a smooth cake about 4 inches across. Place on a generously floured surface and roll the dough into a circle about 12 inches across and $1/8$ inch thick; dust the work surface and the dough with flour as needed to keep the dough from sticking. Transfer to a 9-inch pie pan, then trim and flute the edges. The pie shell is now ready to be filled or baked first and then filled, depending on the recipe.

boiling water pie dough

I know post-Depression-era cooks who swear by this dough, and wouldn't make a pie crust any other way. If you are nervous about making a classic crust, and if blending shortening and flour together using your fingers gives you the willies, this method will liberate you. It goes against anything you've heard about making dough with cold water, and produces a crust that is crisp, flaky, and tender. See the Basic All-American Pie Dough recipe (page 20) for detailed instructions on rolling out and using the dough. This makes enough for a 9-inch pie shell; double the ingredients for a two-crust 9-inch pie.

½ cup vegetable shortening

½ cup boiling water

1½ cups all-purpose flour

½ teaspoon salt

Makes one 9-inch pie shell

Put the shortening in a medium bowl and pour the boiling water over it. Whisk for about 1 minute, until smooth and creamy and about the consistency of sour cream. Add the flour and salt and stir with a fork until you have a ragged-looking dough that barely holds together. Scrape onto a floured surface and push and pat into a round disk 3 to 4 inches across. Wrap in plastic wrap and refrigerate for about an hour. (This is a soft dough and is easier to roll out when it is chilled.)

Sprinkle your work surface, and the top of the dough, generously with flour, and roll out the dough until it is about 1/8 inch thick and about 12 inches across. Transfer to a 9-inch pie pan, then trim and flute the edges. The pie shell is now ready to be filled or baked first and then filled, depending on the recipe.

chocolate nut pie dough

Here is a nutty, cookielike dough that bakes into a crisp pie shell, dandy with any chocolate, peanut butter, or mocha filling. For a rapid-fire dessert, fill the fully baked shell generously with about 8 cups of softened chocolate or vanilla ice cream, or with both flavors swirled together, then return to the freezer until serving time. Accompany with warm butterscotch or chocolate sauce and whipped cream. A knife, dipped for a second in boiling water before each cut, will make slicing the frozen pie easier.

1⅓ cups all-purpose flour

½ cup walnut pieces

¼ cup unsweetened cocoa powder

3 tablespoons sugar

¼ teaspoon salt

½ cup vegetable shortening

½ teaspoon vanilla extract

3 tablespoons milk

Makes one 9-inch pie shell

Combine the flour, walnuts, cocoa, sugar, and salt in a food processor fitted with the metal blade. Whirl together for about 1 minute, until the walnuts are pulverized. Add the shortening and process in 10 to 12 rapid on-off pulses until the mixture looks like coarse, dark crumbs. Add the vanilla and milk and process in 5 or 6 on-off pulses until the dough begins to hold together in a rough, shaggy mass. Scrape the ragged-looking dough onto a generously floured surface and push and pat it into a round cake about 4 inches across. Wrap in plastic wrap and refrigerate for 1 to 2 hours. (This is a soft dough and is easier to roll out when it is chilled.)

Place the dough between 2 large sheets of plastic wrap and roll it into a circle approximately 12 inches in diameter; keep the shape as round as you can, but don't be obsessive about it. Peel off the top sheet of plastic wrap and flip the dough into a 9-inch pie pan, so that the bottom sheet of plastic wrap is up. Peel off the second sheet of plastic wrap. Push and pat the dough evenly into the pan. This cookielike dough is not hurt by handling, and if it tears or breaks, just push it back together. Trim and flute the edges and then fully bake the pie shell, following the instructions on page 22. Since this is a dark dough, the "brownness" visual clue for doneness is not very helpful. You'll know the shell is fully baked when the surface looks dry, with no trace of dampness in the center or around the edges.

jackie's wheat-free pie dough

Some people are unable to digest gluten, and therefore anything made with wheat (and that includes all-purpose flour) is off-limits. For them, most pies are verboten, usually because of the crust. Here is a rice flour dough that makes a rich, sandy-textured crust, and it is wheat free! It is also delicious; I have served it to people who never suspected it did not contain wheat. The composition of this dough makes it easier to handle when made with butter rather than shortening. I especially like it for a fully baked shell, with a cream or chiffon filling. Of course, you must still be knowledgeable of the other ingredients in a recipe, and of your own health needs. This makes enough for a 9-inch pie shell; double the recipe for a two-crust 9-inch pie. The recipe comes from San Francisco writer Jacqueline Mallorca, whose wheatless recipes make gluten-free cooking a pleasure, not a penance.

1 cup brown rice flour

½ cup potato starch flour

½ cup cornstarch

Pinch of salt

1 tablespoon sugar

¾ cup (1½ sticks) cold unsalted butter, cut into ½-inch cubes

1 egg, chilled

Few drops of cold water, if needed

Makes one 9-inch pie shell

In a food processor fitted with the steel blade, combine the rice flour, potato starch, cornstarch, salt, and sugar. Process for a moment to mix the ingredients evenly. Add the butter and process in rapid on-off pulses until the mixture resembles fine meal. With the motor running, add the egg through the food tube, and process just until the dough barely holds together in a ball. If the dough seems dry, add a few drops of water. Dust your work surface with brown rice flour and scrape the dough onto it. Push and pat it into a cake about 4 inches across. At this point, I find the dough easier to roll out if it is wrapped in plastic wrap and refrigerated for about an hour, especially if the kitchen is warm.

Place the dough between 2 large sheets of plastic wrap and roll it into a circle approximately 12 inches in diameter. Rotate the dough and turn it over occasionally to get an even thickness, and try to keep the shape as round as possible. Peel off the top sheet of plastic wrap and flip the dough into a 9-inch pie pan, so that the plastic wrap is up. Peel off the second sheet of plastic wrap. Press and pat the dough evenly into the pan. If it tears, push it back together, and use trimmings from the edge to patch any holes. Trim and flute the edges (see page 22). Place in the freezer for 10 to 15 minutes.

The pie shell is now ready to be filled or baked first and then filled, depending on the recipe. Detailed instructions for fully baked pie shells are on page 22.

crumb crust

A crumb crust will taste better with home-made crumbs, but you can make crumbs from just about any type of crisp, un-iced cookies, so long as they are fresh. A graham cracker or vanilla wafer crust is good with cream cheese fillings, a chocolate crumb crust or biscotti crust pairs well with chocolate and vanilla fillings, and a gingersnap crust will perk up just about anything, particularly pumpkin and chiffon fillings. Crumbs can be made most easily by pulverizing the cookies, broken into pieces, in a food processor or, alternately, by placing the coarsely crumbled cookies in a heavy-duty plastic bag and going over them repeatedly with a rolling pin, lifting and turning the bag every few rolls until you have fine, even crumbs. To make the requisite $1\frac{1}{2}$ cups of crumbs, you will need approximately 14 whole graham crackers, 30 gingersnaps, 50 vanilla wafers, 35 chocolate wafers, or 12 biscotti. Briefly baking a crumb crust enhances its flavor and keeps it crisper after filling, and is worth the little time it takes.

$1\frac{1}{2}$ cups crumbs (if using chocolate wafer cookies, use 2 cups crumbs)

2 tablespoons sugar

Pinch of salt

$\frac{1}{2}$ cup (1 stick) unsalted butter, melted

Makes one 9-inch crumb crust

Combine the crumbs, sugar, and salt in a medium bowl, and stir and toss with a fork. Add the butter and stir vigorously until blended and all the crumbs are moistened. Alternately, you may combine the ingredients in a food processor and whirl until blended.

With your fingers, press and pat the mixture over the bottom and sides of a 9-inch pie pan, building the crumbs up just slightly above the rim of the pan and being careful not to make the sides too thick. Smooth any uneven spots with the back of a spoon.

Before filling the crust, bake it in a preheated 325°F oven for 8 to 10 minutes. Set aside to cool completely before filling.

toasted coconut crust

This really isn't a traditional crust, but rather a buttery shell of toasted coconut, and it's just the ticket for holding any chocolate, coconut, or banana cream filling, or the coffee chiffon filling on page 126.

2 cups shredded, sweetened coconut, toasted (see Note)

½ cup (1 stick) unsalted butter, melted and cooled slightly

1 teaspoon vanilla extract

Pinch of salt

Makes one 9-inch pie shell

Combine the coconut, butter, vanilla, and salt in a medium bowl and stir briskly with a fork until blended. Refrigerate for about 15 minutes, stirring once or twice, or until the coconut has absorbed most of the butter and the mixture begins to hold its shape.

Pat evenly over the bottom and sides of a 9-inch pie pan, building up the coconut just slightly above the rim of the pan. Refrigerate for at least 30 minutes before filling as desired.

Note: To toast packaged coconut, spread it in a shallow baking pan and place in a preheated 350°F oven, stirring occasionally, for 10 to 20 minutes, or until lightly browned.

toppings

A pie is sometimes crowned with a topping, which should not only look nice but also complement the filling underneath. Billows of meringue add an ethereal finish, as well as height, to cream pies and citrus fillings. Whipped cream makes a fast and easy topping for almost any pie, and in spite of its richness, I think it blends particularly well with sweet chocolate, nut, and custard fillings. I've also included a chocolate sauce and a butterscotch sauce, both of which keep for weeks in the refrigerator and can be reheated for serving on a moment's notice.

Meringue making sends many otherwise good bakers into a tailspin when their lustrous topping weeps (beads of liquid sugar rise to the surface) and deflates into a shriveled version of its initial glory. Here is a meringue that holds its shape and stays fluffy without weeping. The step of warming the egg whites and dissolving the sugar—which takes just a few seconds—before beating the meringue is its key to success. I like a generous topping, so this amount will cover any 9-inch pie in a thick, billowy layer. You will need an electric mixer to make it.

meringue topping

²/₃ cup egg whites (about 5 eggs)

½ cup sugar

½ teaspoon cream of tartar

¼ teaspoon salt

½ teaspoon vanilla extract

Combine the egg whites and sugar in a large stainless steel or glass bowl. (I don't recommending using a plastic bowl; it can hold a greasy film that will keep the whites from beating to full volume.) Set the bottom of the bowl over a pan of simmering—not boiling—water. Stir gently for a minute or two, using a spoon or your finger, until the sugar has dissolved and the mixture feels warm. Remove the bowl from the water and add the cream of tartar and salt. Beat at high speed until the whites stand in stiff peaks that droop just slightly when the beater is lifted. Depending on the power and speed of your mixer, this will take 1½ to 3 minutes, more or less, but appearance is a better indicator than time. Beat in the vanilla.

Gently spread the meringue over the pie filling (it's okay if the pie filling is warm), completely covering the filling and making sure the meringue touches the edges of the crust all around. Use the back of a spoon to swirl lofty peaks and deep crevices in the meringue.

To brown the meringue, preheat the broiler and position a rack so that the top of the pie will be about 4 inches from the heat; if you are in doubt, it is better to have it too far from the heat than too close. Put the pie under the broiler until the meringue has glistening, golden streaks and well-browned peaks, 1 or 2 minutes. Don't take your eyes off it, because a few seconds can make a big difference.

Makes meringue topping for one 9-inch pie

Whip cream in a deep, narrow bowl or quart-size measuring cup, using a hand-held rotary beater or a hand-held electric mixer. If you prefer to use a wire whisk, you will, of course, need a bowl large enough to circulate the whisk. Brands of cream vary slightly in fat content. If you have a choice, look at the nutritional analysis, and get the one with the most grams of fat per serving. The higher the fat content, the more easily cream whips, and the longer it stays whipped without deflating.

whipped cream

1 cup heavy (whipping) cream, chilled

4 teaspoons sugar

½ teaspoon vanilla extract

Combine the cream, sugar, and vanilla in a bowl appropriate for your method of whipping, and beat until the cream stands in smooth, fluffy peaks that barely hold their shape. Cover the cream and refrigerate it until needed. It will keep for several hours; if it deflates a bit in the refrigerator, just whip it again until it stands in soft peaks.

Makes about 2 cups whipped cream

You can search high and low, and you won't find a better butterscotch sauce than this, and it is so simple to make. Pass it at the table to spoon over a banana cream, pumpkin, or coconut pie, or any apple or pear pie. Once you try it, there is no going back.

butterscotch sauce

1 cup light or dark brown sugar

½ cup (1 stick) unsalted butter, cut into several pieces

½ cup heavy (whipping) cream

Pinch of salt

½ teaspoon vanilla extract

In a medium saucepan, combine the brown sugar and butter. Cook over moderate heat, stirring or whisking almost constantly, until the butter melts and blends with the sugar. Add the cream and salt and continue whisking until the sauce is smooth. Remove from the heat and stir in the vanilla. For storage, refrigerate what isn't used in a tightly capped jar. The sauce can be reheated gently, either in a saucepan on the stovetop or in a microwave. If it seems a little thick, add another tablespoon or two of cream.

Makes about 1½ cups

Pass warm fudge sauce as a go-along for Black Bottom Pie or for any pie with a coconut or chocolate filling. In a more unlikely match, it is also good dribbled over Orange Chiffon Pie.

chocolate fudge sauce

½ cup (1 stick) unsalted butter

⅔ cup water

4 ounces (4 squares) unsweetened chocolate

1½ cups sugar

¼ cup light corn syrup

Pinch of salt

½ teaspoon vanilla extract

Put the butter and water in a medium saucepan. Bring to a boil over medium-high heat, stirring frequently as the butter melts. Turn the heat to low, then add the chocolate and stir or whisk constantly until the chocolate melts. Don't worry if it looks grainy; it will become smooth later. Add the sugar, corn syrup, and salt and cook gently without boiling, stirring frequently, for about 5 minutes. Remove from the heat and add the vanilla. For storage, refrigerate in a tightly capped jar. The sauce can be reheated gently, either in a saucepan on the stovetop or in a microwave.

Makes about 2½ cups

fruit pies

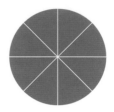

Just reading about fruit pies cannot tell you how good they are; you really have to make one to know. You should experience the perfect balance of sweet, soft fruit filling and crisp crust firsthand to believe it.

If you are used to store-bought pies, you might be surprised when you bake your first fruit pie. Pies turned out in the automated world of bakeries and supermarkets are made to last, and to cut neatly into an even wedge for every serving, so the last slice looks like the first. In other words, a tailored appearance is more important than texture or flavor. On the other hand, a home-baked pie of fresh fruit, with a minimum amount of thickening, does not always cut into neat pieces and can, if the fruit is particularly juicy, be on the messy side. But to my mind, flavor counts more than looks, and you will not be disappointed in the taste. By the way, adding a little butter to a fruit filling, as most of these recipes do, before the top crust is put on, lends a bit of richness and depth. Don't omit it; it makes more of a difference than you might think.

Before baking a two-crust fruit pie, cut several vents, or slits, in the top crust. This enables steam to escape as the fruit cooks and the juices bubble, and prevents the top crust from puffing and possibly bursting. I like pies generously filled with fruit, but in the oven the sweet, bubbling juices from a well-filled pie can sometimes drip over the rim of the crust. To prevent a mess in your oven, I suggest putting a large sheet of heavy duty foil on the rack below the pie or, alternately, setting a shallow baking pan, with about a quarter-inch of water in it, on the lower rack. (Water prevents the pan from scorching and makes cleanup easier.)

Tempting as it might be to cut a fruit pie when it's hot from the oven, it will taste better, and cut more easily, after it cools. When the bottom of the pie pan is faintly warm to your hand, that's the ideal time to make the first slice. I guarantee that if you get a group of adversaries around a table and set a warm peach pie in front of them, they will become friends.

This is easier than many fruit pies because there is no top crust, but rather a sweet, buttery, crunchy, crumbly layer called streusel. Streusel is good over any soft fruit, particularly plums, apricots, and peaches, any of which can be substituted in the following recipe.

fig crumble pie

Basic All-American Pie Dough for a 9-inch pie shell (page 20)

STREUSEL TOPPING

1 cup all-purpose flour

1/2 cup sugar

1 teaspoon ground ginger

1/2 teaspoon ground cinnamon

1/4 teaspoon salt

1/2 cup chopped walnuts

1/2 cup (1 stick) unsalted butter, melted

FIG FILLING

1 1/2 pounds fresh figs, stemmed and sliced 1/3 to 1/2 inch thick, to make about 5 cups

1/4 cup sugar

1 tablespoon fresh lemon juice

1/2 teaspoon vanilla extract

Preheat the oven to 400°F. Roll out the dough and fit it into a 9-inch pie pan. Set aside.

To make the streusel topping, in a medium bowl whisk and toss together the flour, sugar, ginger, cinnamon, and salt. Stir in the walnuts. Add the butter and stir with a fork until you have a damp, crumbly, coarse-looking mixture. Set aside.

To make the filling, place the figs in a large bowl and add the sugar, lemon juice, and vanilla. Using a rubber spatula or your hands, stir and toss gently to coat the figs evenly with the sugar. Spread the fruit in the prepared pie shell. Sprinkle the streusel topping evenly over the fruit.

Bake for about 40 minutes, until the crust and topping are well browned.

Serve warm or at room temperature.

Makes one 9-inch pie

Ginger and almonds pair perfectly with peaches, as well as with apricots and nectarines. All three fruits taste good, and they are easy to work with because they don't need peeling.

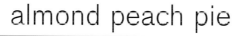 almond peach pie

Basic All-American Pie Dough for a 9-inch two-crust pie (page 20)

⅔ cup sugar

2½ tablespoons cornstarch

⅓ cup blanched almonds, toasted (see Note)

¼ teaspoon salt

2½ to 3 pounds peaches, halved, pitted, and sliced ⅓ to ½ inch thick, to make 6 to 7 cups prepared fruit

2 tablespoons fresh lemon juice

1 tablespoon grated peeled fresh ginger

2 tablespoons unsalted butter, cut into small pieces

Preheat the oven to 425°F. Roll out half of the dough and fit it into a 9-inch pie pan. Roll out the remaining dough for the top crust and set it aside on a sheet of waxed paper.

Place the sugar, cornstarch, almonds, and salt in a blender or food processor. Whirl together until the nuts are pulverized. Put the peaches, lemon juice, and ginger in a large bowl and pour the sugar mixture over them. Toss to combine and coat the fruit evenly. Pile the peaches in the dough-lined pan, mounding the fruit in the center. Scatter the butter over the top.

Put on the top crust, then trim and flute the edges (see page 22). With the point of a sharp knife, slash several vents in the top for steam to escape.

Bake for 25 minutes, then reduce the heat to 350°F and bake for 25 to 30 minutes longer, until the top crust is well browned and the juices are bubbling.

Serve warm or at room temperature.

Note: To toast nuts, spread them in a single layer on a baking sheet and place in a 375°F oven for 7 to 12 minutes, shaking the pan once or twice to turn the nuts and move them about. They are done when they have darkened slightly and have a pleasant, toasty aroma. Alternately, toast by microwaving on high power for 3 to 4 minutes, stirring the nuts and checking them every 30 seconds after the first 2 minutes. Timing varies depending on the amount of nuts and power of the microwave.

Makes one 9-inch pie

Juicy and generous deep-dish pies are baked in casserole or soufflé dishes, with only a top crust. The trick of setting an inverted custard cup in the center of the baking dish before you add the fruit filling is an old one. Not only does it keep the top crust from sagging, it also draws in some of the excess juice, thus lessening the chances of boil-over in the oven. You can also use peaches, apricots, plums, and cherries to make a deep-dish pie. You will need about 3 pounds of any one of these fruits.

deep-dish berry pie

Basic All-American Pie Dough for a 9-inch pie shell (page 20)

1 cup sugar

2½ tablespoons cornstarch

¼ teaspoon salt

6 cups fresh or frozen blackberries, blueberries, or boysenberries, about 2¼ pounds (it is not necessary to thaw frozen berries)

1 tablespoon fresh lemon juice

2 tablespoons unsalted butter, cut into small pieces

Preheat the oven to 425°F. You will need a 7- to 8-cup baking dish that is about 3 inches deep with fairly straight sides. Roll out the dough to a shape about 1 inch larger than the top of the baking dish. Set the rolled-out dough aside on a sheet of waxed paper.

In a large bowl, stir together the sugar, cornstarch, and salt until evenly mixed. Add the berries and lemon juice and toss until the fruit is evenly coated with the sugar mixture. Set an ovenproof cup, such as a 4- to 6-ounce ramekin or custard cup, upside down in the middle of the baking dish. Fill the baking dish with the berries, then dot the top with the butter.

Set the rolled-out dough over the berries, leaving about 1 inch of overhang all around; trim away any excess. Gently press the dough into the dish around the sides, and fold the overhanging dough under itself to make a double-thick rim around the edge. Flute the rim (see page 22). Slash a few vents in the top to allow steam to escape.

Bake for about 50 minutes, until the juices are bubbling and the crust is well browned.

Serve warm or at room temperature, taking care to work gently around the custard cup or ramekin as you scoop the pie onto plates.

Makes one deep-dish pie, serving 6

This system of slightly cooking the berries in sugar and water and then spreading them over a sour cream custard—which will remind you of cheesecake—works equally well with pitted cherries.

blackberry sour cream pie

Basic All-American Pie Dough (page 20) or Crumb Crust for a 9-inch pie shell, made with graham crackers or gingersnaps (page 32)

SOUR CREAM CUSTARD LAYER

1½ cups sour cream

½ cup sugar

3 eggs

1½ teaspoons vanilla extract

Pinch of salt

BLACKBERRY LAYER

½ cup sugar

½ cup water

2 cups fresh or frozen blackberries, about 12 ounces (it is not necessary to thaw frozen berries)

1 tablespoon cornstarch

1 tablespoon water

If you are using pie dough, preheat the oven to 425°F. Roll out the dough and fit it into a 9-inch pie pan, then trim and flute the edges. Bake the pie shell fully, following the instructions on page 22. If you are using a crumb crust, form and bake the crust as directed in the recipe. Cool either crust completely before filling.

To make the sour cream custard, preheat the oven to 325°F. In a medium bowl, whisk together the sour cream, sugar, eggs, vanilla, and salt until smooth. Pour into the cooled pie shell and bake for 35 to 40 minutes, or until the custard is set and doesn't have a liquidy jiggle when the pan is moved. Remove from the oven and cool to room temperature. If you want, refrigerate the pie for several hours at this point, before spreading the berries over the custard.

To prepare the berries, in a medium-sized saucepan, combine the sugar and water and bring to a boil over medium-high heat, stirring until the sugar dissolves. Reduce the heat to low and add the berries. Cook gently for about 5 minutes, stirring occasionally, until the berries soften and exude some juice. In a small cup or bowl, stir the cornstarch and water together until smooth, then add to the simmering berry mixture and boil gently for about 1 minute, until slightly thickened. Set aside to cool for about 30 minutes, stirring occasionally.

Spoon the berries over the custard, spreading them all the way to the edge. Refrigerate for about 2 hours, or overnight if you wish, before serving.

Makes one 9-inch pie

A thin layer of orange-flavored cream cheese topped with a soft blueberry compote, this pie is like a cheesecake, but less rich and filling. For a faster, more streamlined pie, use whole, uncooked raspberries, tossed with a little sugar, in place of the blueberry topping.

orange blueberry pie

Crumb Crust for a 9-inch pie shell, made with graham crackers (page 32)

ORANGE CREAM CHEESE CUSTARD

2½ teaspoons (1 envelope) unflavored gelatin

½ cup sugar

1 cup fresh orange juice

12 ounces (1½ cups) cream cheese, at room temperature

2 tablespoons grated orange zest

2 tablespoons orange liqueur (optional)

BLUEBERRY TOPPING

2 cups fresh or frozen blueberries, 8 to 10 ounces (it is not necessary to thaw frozen berries)

⅓ cup water

⅓ cup sugar

1 tablespoon grated orange zest

1½ tablespoons cornstarch

2 tablespoons water

Form and bake the crumb crust as directed in the recipe. Cool completely before filling.

To make the custard, in a large bowl whisk together the gelatin and sugar. Bring the orange juice to a boil in a small saucepan, then pour it over the gelatin mixture and stir until the sugar dissolves. Let stand for about 5 minutes, stirring occasionally. Add the cream cheese and orange zest and whisk or beat until smooth; a hand-held rotary beater or electric mixer on low speed is useful for this. If you wish, stir in the orange liqueur. Pour into the prepared crust and refrigerate until set, about 2 hours, or overnight if desired.

To make the blueberry topping, in a medium saucepan combine the blueberries, water, sugar, and orange zest. Bring to a boil over medium-high heat, then reduce the heat and simmer gently for about 3 minutes; the berries should soften slightly, and some of their skins will pop. In a small bowl, mix together the cornstarch and water, and add it into the berries. Simmer for about 1 minute longer, stirring constantly, until slightly thickened. Remove from the heat and set aside to cool until tepid.

Spoon the berries over the custard and refrigerate for at least 1 hour before serving.

Makes one 9-inch pie

Some recipes transcend their simple ingredients: You can't imagine how good they are until you taste the finished dish. Shaker lemon pie, also known as Ohio lemon pie, is such a recipe. With a sweet, intense flavor, it's more lemon slices than anything, held together in a tender egg custard. A sharp knife and a long sojourn in the sugar for the lemon slices to tenderize the lemon skins are the secrets to its success.

shaker lemon pie

3 lemons

2 cups sugar

Basic All-American Pie Dough for a 9-inch two-crust pie (page 20)

4 eggs, beaten

Rinse the lemons well, then pat them dry with paper towels. Cut off and discard the ends. Using the fine holes of a grater, grate the zest from the lemons; you need only a tablespoon or two, so don't worry about removing every bit. Put the zest into a large bowl.

Working with a very sharp knife, preferably one with a long, thin blade, slice 2½ of the lemons as thinly as you can (at best, you should be able to read through a slice), poking out the seeds as they appear. Put the lemon slices into the bowl with the zest. Squeeze the juice from the remaining lemon half and add it to the bowl, along with the sugar. Toss to combine and coat the lemon slices evenly, then cover with plastic wrap and let stand at room temperature for 3 to 5 hours.

Preheat the oven to 450°F. Roll out half the dough for the bottom crust and fit it into a 9-inch pie pan. Roll out the remaining dough for the top crust and set it aside on a sheet of waxed paper.

Add the eggs to the lemon mixture and stir until evenly mixed. Pour into the dough-lined pan. Put the top crust in place, then trim and flute the edges (see page 22). With the point of a sharp knife, slash a few vents in the top for steam to escape.

Bake for 15 minutes, then lower the heat to 375°F and bake for 30 to 40 minutes more, until the crust is lightly browned and a knife inserted into one of the vents comes out clean, or with just a translucent film of filling on it. Cool to room temperature before serving. Refrigerate any leftover pie.

Makes one 9-inch pie

With their soft, unctuous texture, pears just seem made to absorb the caramel-like blend of butter and brown sugar. This pie takes a bit of time to prepare, and if you aren't in the mood to make pie dough, the pears are delicious on their own, with ice cream and cookies. When fruit tastes this good, there is no need for spices.

caramelized pear pie

6 to 7 firm but ripe pears, preferably Boscs, 2½ to 3 pounds

¼ cup (½ stick) unsalted butter

⅔ cup brown sugar

2 tablespoons fresh lemon juice

Pinch of salt

2 tablespoons rum

Basic All-American Pie Dough for a 9-inch two-crust pie (page 20)

Peel, halve, and core the pears, then cut them into crosswise slices about ⅓ inch thick (crosswise slices hold their shape better than lengthwise slices). In a large skillet over medium-high heat, melt the butter and brown sugar together, stirring frequently. Add the pears, lemon juice, and salt. In a moment, the pears will exude a lot of juice. Continue cooking over moderate heat, stirring frequently with a wooden spoon or spatula, until the juices have mostly evaporated and the pears are coated in a thick, syrupy, caramel-like sauce. Depending on the ripeness and juiciness of the pears, and the size of your pan, this will take 10 to 20 minutes. Stir in the rum and cook for about 1 minute longer. Set aside to cool while you roll out the dough.

Preheat the oven to 425°F. Roll out half of the dough for the bottom crust and fit it into a 9-inch pie pan. Roll out the remaining dough for the top crust and set it aside on a sheet of waxed paper.

Spoon the pears, along with any sauce, into the dough-lined pan. Cover with the top crust, then trim and flute the edges (see page 22). With the point of a sharp knife, slash a few vents in the top for steam to escape.

Bake for 25 minutes, then reduce the heat to 350°F. Continue baking for 20 to 25 minutes longer, until the crust is well browned.

Serve warm or at room temperature.

Makes one 9-inch pie

A mid-1930s Toll House cookbook, from the famous Massachusetts inn of the same name, includes a recipe for Honolulu Date Squares. It's an old-fashioned cookie with a gooey date filling enclosed in a rich, cookielike crust. This pie is based on those bars. If you are timid about dough making, note that this pie is made with a press-in-the-pan crust and a sprinkled-on topping that require no rolling pin. Some dates feel moist and sticky; others are naturally firmer and drier. Depending on yours, you might need to use more water in cooking.

date bar pie

DATE FILLING

3 cups whole pitted dates, about 12 ounces

⅓ cup brown sugar

¾ cup water, plus more if needed

1 Golden Delicious apple, peeled, cored, and coarsely grated

⅛ teaspoon salt

3 tablespoons rum

COOKIE CRUST

¾ cup all-purpose flour

½ teaspoon plus ¼ teaspoon baking soda

¼ teaspoon salt

1½ cups uncooked oatmeal

½ cup brown sugar

10 tablespoons (1¼ sticks) unsalted butter, melted

To make the date filling, using a sharp knife or scissors, coarsely cut the dates. (Running the blade under cold water periodically will help when you are cutting sticky fruit.) Put them in a medium, heavy-bottomed saucepan and add the brown sugar, ¾ cup water, apple, and salt. Cook over moderate heat, stirring frequently, until the mixture is quite thick; a blob of it lifted in a spoon should be moist but hold its shape. Set aside to cool for about 15 minutes, then stir in the rum. If at this point the mixture appears very stiff and sticky, stir in another tablespoon or two of water.

Preheat the oven to 375°F. Coat the inside of a 9-inch pie pan with nonstick cooking spray, or smear it with a thin film of butter.

While the dates cool, prepare the cookie crust. Combine the flour, baking soda, and salt and sift them together into a large bowl. Add the oatmeal and brown sugar and stir together with a fork or whisk. Add the butter and stir briskly until you have a crumbly looking mixture. Press 1 cup of the mixture over the bottom (not the sides) of the prepared pan. Spread with the date filling, then distribute the remaining crust mixture over the top; it will be in irregular bits, so don't worry about making it perfectly even. Bake for about 40 minutes, until the bits of topping have browned and spread slightly.

Serve warm or at room temperature.

Makes one 9-inch pie

Instead of a top crust, this pie has a quickly made, crunchy topping of streusel, so you get the pleasures of a fruit pie, but with a little less work. The brief preliminary cooking in a little butter enhances the apricots' natural flavor. Streusel is also very good over peaches, which can be substituted in this pie.

apricot crumble pie

Basic All-American Pie Dough for a 9-inch pie shell (page 20)

STREUSEL TOPPING

¼ cup (½ stick) unsalted butter, at room temperature

½ cup brown sugar

½ cup all-purpose flour

½ cup uncooked oatmeal

½ teaspoon ground nutmeg

¼ teaspoon salt

APRICOT FILLING

2 tablespoons unsalted butter

2¼ pounds apricots, pitted and quartered, to make about 6 cups prepared fruit

½ cup sugar

2 tablespoons all-purpose flour

Pinch of salt

Preheat the oven to 375°F. Roll out the dough and fit it into a 9-inch pie pan, then trim and flute the edges (see page 22).

To make the streusel topping, put the butter and sugar in a medium bowl and beat them together, using a large wooden spoon or a rubber spatula. Add the flour, oatmeal, nutmeg, and salt and, using your fingers, blend the ingredients together until you have a mixture that looks like fine, irregular crumbs. Set aside.

To prepare the filling, melt the butter in a large skillet set over moderate heat. When hot, add the apricots and cook, stirring occasionally, for about 5 minutes. In the meantime, stir together the sugar, flour, and salt in a small bowl. Add the sugar mixture to the fruit and cook, stirring occasionally, until the juices have thickened and the fruit has softened, 3 to 5 minutes more. Spoon the hot fruit into the prepared pie shell. Sprinkle the streusel mixture evenly over the top.

Bake for 40 to 45 minutes, until the juices are bubbling and the topping is well browned.

Serve warm or at room temperature.

Makes one 9-inch pie

There are many types of plums, and just about any of them, if firm and flavorful, will make a nice pie. But if I had to pick my favorite, it would be purple Santa Rosa plums, not overly ripe. When you see them, grab all you can and enjoy them (they also make wonderful jam), because they are scarce and their season is short. Regardless of variety, plums are apt to be very juicy, and you would be wise to set a foil-lined baking sheet on the oven rack under the pie to catch any drips.

 # plum pie

Basic All-American Pie Dough for a 9-inch two-crust pie (page 20)

2½ tablespoons cornstarch

1⅓ cups sugar

¼ teaspoon salt

3 pounds plums, halved, pitted, and sliced about ½ inch thick, to make about 8 cups prepared fruit

1 tablespoon fresh lemon juice

2 tablespoons unsalted butter, cut into small pieces

Preheat the oven to 425°F. Roll out half of the dough for the bottom crust and fit it into a 9-inch pie pan. Roll out the remaining dough for the top crust and set it aside on a sheet of waxed paper.

In a large bowl, combine the cornstarch, sugar, and salt, using a fork or a whisk. Add the plums and lemon juice and toss together until the fruit is coated with the sugar mixture. Pile into the dough-lined pan, mounding the fruit slightly in the center. Scatter the butter over the fruit. Put on the top crust, then press firmly all around the edges to seal. Trim and flute the edges (see page 22). Using the point of a sharp knife, cut several vents in the top for steam to escape.

Bake for 25 minutes, then reduce the heat to 350°F and continue baking for about 30 minutes longer, until the juices are bubbling and the crust is nicely browned.

Serve warm or at room temperature.

Makes one 9-inch pie

Rhubarb, like celery, can sometimes be fibrous along the top surface. If your stalks seem a little tough or stringy as you slice them, just shave them with a vegetable peeler first. Use only the rhubarb stalks in cooking, not the leaves.

cherry rhubarb pie

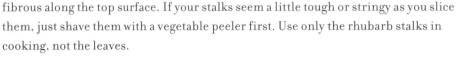

Basic All-American Pie Dough for a 9-inch two-crust pie (page 20)

1 cup plus 1 tablespoon sugar

2 tablespoons cornstarch

¼ teaspoon salt

12 to 14 ounces rhubarb stalks, sliced into ½-inch pieces, to make 2 to 2½ cups

4 cups pitted sweet cherries, 1 to 1¼ pounds

3 or 4 drops almond extract

2 tablespoons unsalted butter, cut in small pieces

Preheat the oven to 425°F. Roll out half of the dough for the bottom crust and fit it into a 9-inch pie pan. Roll out the remaining dough for the top crust and set it aside on a sheet of waxed paper.

In a large bowl, stir together 1 cup of the sugar, cornstarch, and salt. Add the rhubarb, cherries, and almond extract and toss to coat the fruit evenly. Pile the mixture in the dough-lined pan, then scatter the butter over the filling. Cover with the top crust, then trim and flute the edges (see page 22). With the point of a sharp knife, cut a few vents in the top for steam to escape.

Bake for 25 minutes, then reduce the heat to 350°F. Bake for another 15 minutes, then sprinkle the top with the remaining tablespoon of sugar. Bake for 15 to 20 minutes longer, or until the juices are bubbling and the crust is browned.

Serve warm or at room temperature.

Makes one 9-inch pie

Pineapple is so sweet and aromatic,
why relegate it to upside-down cakes and baked hams? Further, apricots and pineapple
are so companionable that the resulting flavor seems greater than the sum of its parts.

pineapple apricot pie

Basic All-American Pie Dough for a 9-inch two-crust pie (page 20)

1 cup sugar

2½ tablespoons cornstarch

¼ teaspoon salt

¼ teaspoon ground cardamom or cinnamon

3 cups pineapple chunks, well drained, either fresh or canned

12 to 14 ounces apricots, pitted and quartered, to make about 3 cups prepared fruit

2 tablespoons unsalted butter, cut into small pieces

Preheat the oven to 425°F. Roll out half of the dough for the bottom crust and fit it into a 9-inch pie pan. Roll out the remaining dough for the top crust and set it aside on a sheet of waxed paper.

In a small bowl, stir together the sugar, cornstarch, salt, and cardamom. Set aside.

Put the pineapple chunks in a large bowl and crush them slightly with a potato masher or a large fork—they should be broken up but not crushed. Add the apricots and the reserved sugar mixture, and toss to combine and coat the fruit evenly. Pour the fruit mixture into the dough-lined pan and scatter the butter over the filling. Cover with the top crust, then trim and flute the edges (see page 22). With the point of a sharp knife, slash a few vents in the top for steam to escape.

Bake for 25 minutes, then reduce the heat to 350°F and continue baking for 30 to 35 minutes longer, until the crust is well browned and the juices are bubbling.

Serve warm or at room temperature.

Makes one 9-inch pie

Although rhubarb is rather homely, what it lacks in appearance it makes up for in taste. One friend commented that this pie "smells like summer," and it will indeed win you over with its enticing aroma while baking and its pure flavor. Strawberries and rhubarb are a familiar, nostalgic combination, yet to my mind other berries, particularly blackberries and boysenberries, taste even better. This is quite a juicy pie and is apt to drip in the oven, so place a large sheet of foil on the rack below to catch any mess.

rhubarb berry pie

Basic All-American Pie Dough for a 9-inch two-crust pie (page 20)

1⅓ cups sugar

2½ tablespoons cornstarch

2 teaspoons grated lemon zest

¼ teaspoon salt

2½ cups fresh berries, such as blackberries, raspberries, boysenberries, or sliced strawberries

1¼ pounds rhubarb stalks, peeled if stringy (see headnote, page 58) and cut into ½-inch pieces, to make about 4 cups

2 tablespoons unsalted butter, cut into small bits

Preheat the oven to 425°F. Roll out half of the dough for the bottom crust and fit it into a 9-inch pie pan. Roll out the remaining dough for the top crust and set it aside on a sheet of waxed paper.

In a small bowl, using a fork or whisk, stir together the sugar, cornstarch, lemon zest, and salt. Set aside.

In a large bowl, toss the berries and rhubarb together. Add the sugar mixture and toss to combine and coat the fruit evenly. Pile the mixture into the prepared pie pan, mounding the fruit in the center. Scatter the butter over the filling. Put on the top crust, then trim and flute the edges (see page 22). With the point of a sharp knife, cut a few vents in the top for steam to escape.

Bake for 20 minutes, then reduce the heat to 350°F and continue baking for 35 to 40 minutes longer, until the top crust is well browned and the juices are bubbling.

Serve warm or at room temperature.

Makes one 9-inch pie

Cut into this pie when it has cooled completely to room temperature, to allow the tart rhubarb to imbibe the sweet, flavorful juices produced during baking. Then serve it with a sweet go-along, like whipped cream or ice cream. (If your rhubarb stalks seem particularly fibrous, see the headnote on page 58.)

rhubarb pie

Basic All-American Pie Dough for a 9-inch two-crust pie (page 20)

1½ cups sugar

3 tablespoons cornstarch

¼ teaspoon salt

2½ pounds rhubarb stalks, sliced into ½-inch pieces, to make 6 to 6¼ cups

½ teaspoon vanilla extract

2 tablespoons unsalted butter, cut into small pieces

Preheat the oven to 425°F. Roll out half the dough for the bottom crust and fit it into a 9-inch pie pan. Roll out the remaining dough for the top crust and set it aside on a sheet of waxed paper.

In a large bowl, stir together the sugar, cornstarch, and salt until evenly blended. Add the rhubarb and vanilla and toss to coat the rhubarb evenly. (After tossing for a minute or so, if you still have any dry sugar mixture in the bowl, just scoop it in with the rest of the filling and it will dissolve during baking.) Pile the mixture in the dough-lined pan, mounding it in the center, then scatter the butter over the filling. Cover with the top crust, then trim and flute the edges (see page 22). With the point of a sharp knife, cut several vents in the top for steam to escape.

Bake for 25 minutes, then reduce the oven temperature to 350°F. Bake for about 40 minutes longer, or until the juices are bubbling, the crust is browned, and a sharp knife inserted through one of the vents pierces the rhubarb easily.

Serve at room temperature.

Makes one 9-inch pie

My friend Michael Procopio, who has good taste in food and wine, thought apples and whiskey made a better-tasting, and much more American, blend than the apples and red wine I'd originally used in this pie. He was right. This is a decidedly adult dessert, and if you have some bourbon left, throw a splash into the whipped cream that tops each slice.

whiskey apple pie

Basic All-American Pie Dough for a 9-inch two-crust pie (page 20)

6 or 7 Golden Delicious Apples, 2½ to 3 pounds

⅓ cup sugar

2 tablespoons all-purpose flour

½ teaspoon ground cinnamon

½ teaspoon ground nutmeg

¼ teaspoon salt

½ cup bourbon whiskey

2 tablespoons lemon juice

2 tablespoons unsalted butter, cut into small pieces

Whipped Cream (page 39), for serving

Preheat the oven to 425°F. Roll out half the dough for the bottom crust and fit it into a 9-inch pie pan. Roll out the remaining dough for the top crust and set it aside on a sheet of waxed paper.

To make the filling, peel, halve, and core the apples, then cut them into slices ¼ to ⅓ inch thick; you should have 7 to 8 cups. Set aside. In a saucepan of at least 4-quart capacity, whisk together the sugar, flour, cinnamon, nutmeg, and salt. Add the bourbon and lemon juice and whisk until evenly blended. Place over medium-high heat and cook, whisking frequently, until the mixture boils and thickens slightly. Add the apples and stir and toss to coat them evenly with the bourbon mixture. Continue cooking for about 3 minutes, stirring constantly. Set aside for about 20 minutes, stirring once or twice.

Pour the apple mixture into the dough-lined pan, mounding it slightly in the center. Scatter the butter over the fruit. Cover with the top crust, then trim and flute the edges (see page 22). With the point of a sharp knife, slash several vents in the top for steam to escape.

Bake for 25 minutes, then reduce the oven temperature to 350°F and continue baking for about 45 minutes longer, or until the crust is browned, the juices are bubbling, and the fruit is tender when pierced with a knife inserted through one of the vents.

Serve warm or at room temperature, with whipped cream.

Makes one 9-inch pie

Rather than a top crust, here tender apple slices are covered with a crumbly, nutty oatmeal topping. Precooking the apples brings out their flavor and imparts a buttery sweetness that is delicious. Firm, ripe Bosc pears can be used with equal success in this pie.

apple crisp pie

Basic All-American Pie Dough for a 9-inch pie shell (page 20)

BUTTERY OATMEAL TOPPING

¼ cup (½ stick) unsalted butter, at room temperature

½ cup brown sugar

½ cup all-purpose flour

½ cup uncooked oatmeal

½ cup chopped walnuts

½ teaspoon ground cinnamon

¼ teaspoon salt

APPLE FILLING

6 to 7 Golden Delicious apples, about 3 pounds

¼ cup (½ stick) unsalted butter

½ cup sugar

Pinch of salt

1 tablespoon fresh lemon juice

Roll out the dough and fit it into a 9-inch pie pan, then trim and flute the edges (see page 22). Set aside.

To make the topping, put the butter, brown sugar, flour, oatmeal, walnuts, cinnamon, and salt in a large bowl. Using your fingertips or a pastry blender, blend the ingredients together until the mixture looks like coarse crumbs. Don't worry about overblending the ingredients; just keep at it until you have a coarse, crumbly mixture. Set aside.

To make the filling, peel, halve, and core the apples, then cut them into slices ¼ to ⅓ inch thick. Set aside. In a large skillet, combine the butter, sugar, and salt and place over medium-high heat. Cook, stirring frequently, until the butter has melted and blended with the sugar, 2 to 3 minutes. Add the apple slices and lemon juice. The apples will almost immediately exude some juice.

(Pears, if you are using them here, will exude quite a lot of juice.) Continue to cook, stirring frequently, until the apple slices are tender and translucent and any juices have mostly evaporated, about 15 minutes. Remove from the heat and set aside to cool for about 20 minutes, stirring once or twice.

Preheat the oven to 450°F while the apples are cooling.

Spread the apples in the prepared pie shell, then sprinkle the oatmeal topping evenly over the fruit. Bake for 10 minutes, then reduce the heat to 350°F and continue baking for about 30 minutes longer, until the topping and the edges of the crust are browned. Depending on the fruit, you might also see some syrupy juices bubbling around the crust.

Serve warm or at room temperature.

Makes one 9-inch pie

Cranberries, with their glistening, scarlet color and tart flavor, have so much going for them, whether they are in breads and muffins, a chilled relish, or this autumn pie.

apple cranberry pie

Basic All-American Pie Dough for a 9-inch two-crust pie (page 20)

1 cup sugar

2 tablespoons all-purpose flour

½ teaspoon ground cinnamon

¼ teaspoon salt

5 apples, preferably Golden Delicious, peeled, halved, cored, and sliced about ¼-inch thick, 2 to 2½ pounds

1 cup cranberries, fresh or frozen (it is not necessary to thaw frozen berries)

½ cup dried currants

2 tablespoons fresh lemon juice

2 tablespoons unsalted butter, cut into small pieces

Preheat the oven to 425°F. Roll out half of the dough for the bottom crust and fit it into a 9-inch pie pan. Roll out the remaining dough for the top crust and set it aside on a sheet of waxed paper.

In a large bowl stir together the sugar, flour, cinnamon, and salt until evenly mixed. Add the apples, cranberries, currants, and lemon juice. Using your hands, toss and mix until all the fruit is evenly coated with the sugar mixture. Pour the fruit into the dough lined pan, mounding it slightly in the center. Scatter the butter over the fruit. Cover with the top crust, then trim and flute the edges (see page 22). With the point of a sharp knife, slash several vents in the top for steam to escape.

Bake for 25 minutes, then reduce the heat to 350°F and continue baking for 40 to 50 minutes longer, or until the crust is browned, the juices are bubbling, and the fruit seems tender when pierced with a knife through one of the vents.

Serve warm or at room temperature.

Makes one 9-inch pie

Apple pie is such a symbol of Americana, it is easy to assume that everyone knows how to make one. Of course, this isn't true, so here is a version that has worked well for me. I like Golden Delicious apples because they taste good in a pie, they hold their shape, and they cook more quickly than other varieties, meaning that the apples are tender before the crust gets too dark.

apple pie

Basic All-American Pie Dough for a 9-inch two-crust pie (page 20)

³/₄ cup sugar

2 tablespoons all-purpose flour

¹/₂ teaspoon ground cinnamon

¹/₄ teaspoon ground nutmeg

¹/₄ teaspoon salt

6 to 7 Golden Delicious apples, peeled, halved, cored, and sliced about ¹/₄ inch thick, to make about 8 cups prepared apples, about 3 pounds

2 tablespoons fresh lemon juice

2 tablespoons unsalted butter, cut into small pieces

Preheat the oven to 425°F. Roll out half of the dough for the bottom crust and fit it into a 9-inch pie pan. Roll out the remaining dough for the top crust and set aside on a sheet of waxed paper.

In a small cup or bowl, stir together the sugar, flour, cinnamon, nutmeg, and salt until completely mixed. Set aside.

Put the apple slices in a large bowl, add the lemon juice, and toss with your hands to coat the apples with the juice. Add the sugar mixture and continue tossing until the apples are evenly coated. Pile the apples into the dough-lined pan, mounding them slightly in the center. Scatter the butter over the apples. Put on the top crust, then trim and flute the edges (see page 22). With the point of a sharp knife, cut several vents in the top for steam to escape.

Bake for 25 minutes, then reduce the heat to 350°F and continue baking for about 45 minutes longer, until the crust is browned, the juices are bubbling, and the apples are tender when pierced with a knife inserted through one of the vents.

Serve warm or at room temperature.

Makes one 9-inch pie

When it's high time for fruit pies, head for the peaches. A good peach pie can make you famous, I think, and if you want to know why, just taste the first bite. I used to take the time to peel peaches, until a first-rate baker I know told me that she never did. I'd assumed that peeled peaches were better, but as long as the skins are tender, it doesn't matter.

peach pie

Basic All-American Pie Dough for a 9-inch two-crust pie (page 20)

²/₃ cup plus 1 tablespoon sugar

¹/₃ cup all-purpose flour

¹/₄ teaspoon ground nutmeg

¹/₄ teaspoon salt

3 tablespoons fresh lemon juice

3 pounds peaches, halved, pitted, and sliced ¹/₃ to ¹/₂ inch thick, to make about 7 cups prepared fruit

2 tablespoons unsalted butter, cut into small pieces

Preheat the oven to 425°F. Roll out half of the dough for the bottom crust and fit it into a 9-inch pie pan. Roll out the remaining dough for the top crust and set it aside on a sheet of waxed paper.

In a large bowl, stir together ²/₃ cup of the sugar, the flour, nutmeg, and salt with a fork or whisk until evenly mixed. Add the lemon juice and peaches and toss until the fruit is completely coated with the sugar mixture. Pile the peaches in the dough-lined pan, mounding them slightly in the center. Scatter the butter over the fruit.

Put on the top crust, then trim and flute the edges (see page 22). With the point of a sharp knife, cut several vents in the top for steam to escape.

Bake for 25 minutes, then reduce the heat to 350°F. Bake for another 15 minutes, then rapidly sprinkle the remaining 1 tablespoon sugar over the top of the pie. Continue baking for about 15 minutes longer, or until the crust is golden brown and you see juices bubbling through the vents.

Serve warm or at room temperature.

Makes one 9-inch pie

Baking a cherry pie is easy; pitting the cherries is a chore. An inexpensive cherry pitter, which works on the same principle as a one-hole paper punch and can be found at many hardware and cookware shops, makes relatively quick work of the task. Sweet cherries result in a grand pie, as do sour cherries on the rare occasion that you can find them. (If you use sour cherries, increase the sugar to 1¼ cups.) Farmers' markets are a good place to find locally grown cherries.

cherry pie

Basic All-American Pie Dough for a 9-inch two-crust pie (page 20)

⅔ cup sugar

3 tablespoons cornstarch

¼ teaspoon salt

6 cups pitted sweet cherries, about 2 pounds

6 to 8 drops almond extract

2 tablespoons unsalted butter, cut into small pieces

Preheat the oven to 425°F. Roll out half the dough for the bottom crust and fit it into a 9-inch pie pan. Roll out the remaining dough for the top crust and set it aside on a sheet of waxed paper.

In a large bowl, stir together the sugar, cornstarch, and salt until evenly mixed. Add the cherries and almond extract and toss to coat the fruit evenly with the sugar mixture. Pile the fruit in the dough-lined pan (if any dry sugar mixture remains in the bowl, just sprinkle it over the fruit), then scatter the butter over the filling. Cover with the top crust, then trim and flute the edges (see page 22). With the point of a sharp knife, cut several vents in the top for steam to escape.

Bake for 25 minutes, then reduce the oven temperature to 350°F. Bake for 25 to 30 minutes more, or until the juices are bubbling and the crust is well browned. A sharp knife inserted into the filling through one of the vents should pierce the cherries easily.

Serve warm or at room temperature.

Makes one 9-inch pie

It doesn't matter whether you use fresh or properly frozen berries here; you would be hard-pressed to tell the difference when you taste the pie. In the oven, sweetened berries yield a lot of syrupy, bubbling juices, so it's a smart idea to put a foil-lined baking sheet on the rack below the pie while it bakes.

 # berry pie

Basic All-American Pie Dough for a 9-inch two-crust pie (page 20)

1 cup sugar

2½ tablespoons cornstarch

¼ teaspoon salt

6 cups blackberries, boysenberries, or blueberries, about 1¾ pounds (if using frozen berries, don't thaw them)

2 tablespoons unsalted butter, cut into small pieces

Preheat the oven to 425°F. Roll out half the dough for the bottom crust and fit it into a 9-inch pie pan. Roll out the remaining dough for the top crust and set it aside on a sheet of waxed paper.

In a large bowl, stir together the sugar, cornstarch, and salt. Add the berries and toss to coat them evenly. Pile the mixture in the dough-lined pan, mounding the fruit slightly in the center, then scatter the butter over the filling. Cover with the top crust, then trim and flute the edges (see page 22). With the point of a sharp knife, cut a few vents in the top for steam to escape.

Bake for 25 minutes, then reduce the heat to 350°F. Bake for about 35 minutes longer, or until the juices are bubbling and the crust is browned.

Serve warm or at room temperature.

Makes one 9-inch pie

At holiday time everybody needs a couple of good pies that are synonymous with the season. This recipe and the one that follows will round out any festive fall or winter dinner. Both pies go together relatively easily (a plus for a holiday dessert), and they keep their goodness even if you make them a day ahead. If this combination of sweet raisins and tart cranberries seems odd, give it a try anyway. You'll find that the fruits blend beautifully to make a glistening filling that is not overly rich.

cranberry raisin pie

2 cups raisins

Basic All-American Pie Dough for a 9-inch two-crust pie (page 20)

1 cup sugar

2 tablespoons all-purpose flour

Pinch of salt

4 cups (one 12-ounce bag) fresh cranberries

¼ cup orange liqueur or sweet sherry

1 tablespoon grated orange zest

Put the raisins in a large bowl, cover them with water, and let soak for 2 to 3 hours. Pour the raisins into a colander or large strainer to drain, shaking them to remove excess water. Set aside.

Preheat the oven to 425°F. Roll out half of the dough for the bottom crust and fit it into a 9-inch pie pan. Roll out the remaining dough for the top crust and set it aside on a sheet of waxed paper.

Stir together the sugar, flour, and salt in a large, dry bowl until the flour disappears. Add the raisins, cranberries, orange liqueur, and orange zest, then stir and toss together until the fruit is evenly coated with the sugar mixture. Put the fruit into the dough-lined pan, mounding it slightly in the center. Put the top crust in place, then trim and flute the edges (see page 22). With the point of a sharp knife, cut several vents in the top for steam to escape.

Bake for 15 minutes, then reduce the heat to 350°F and continue baking for 45 to 50 minutes longer, until the crust is browned and the juices are bubbling.

Serve warm or at room temperature.

Makes one 9-inch pie

I don't see many people making mincemeat from scratch today; it is indeed a labor of love and often a family effort. Store-bought mincemeat, in my experience can be very sweet and starchy, and it contains no meat to boot! Blending it with other ingredients rounds out its flavor and improves the texture. This is much richer than the preceding cranberry pie; in fact, most people compare it to traditional mincemeat.

cranberry mincemeat pie

Basic All-American Pie Dough for a 9-inch two-crust pie (page 20)

½ cup sugar

1 tablespoon all-purpose flour

2 to 2½ cups prepared mincemeat

2 cups fresh cranberries

2 Golden Delicious apples, peeled, cored, and coarsely chopped

2 tablespoons unsalted butter, cut into small pieces

Preheat the oven to 450°F. Roll out half of the dough for the bottom crust and fit it into a 9-inch pie pan. Roll out the remaining dough for the top crust and set it aside on a sheet of waxed paper.

In a large bowl, stir together the sugar and flour until the flour disappears. Add the mincemeat, cranberries, and apples, then stir and toss until thoroughly mixed. Pour the mixture into the dough-lined pan and scatter the butter over the filling. Put the top crust in place, then trim and flute the edges (see page 22). With the point of a sharp knife, cut several vents in the top for steam to escape.

Bake for 15 minutes, then reduce the heat to 350°F and bake for 45 to 50 minutes longer, or until the crust is browned and the juices are bubbling.

Serve warm or at room temperature.

Makes one 9-inch pie

Raw quince is quite harsh and tannic, but poaching it in a sweet, spiced sugar syrup transforms it into a delicate treat. Here, the tender slices with a buttery texture are paired with whipped cream and butterscotch sauce in a spicy gingersnap crust. The fruit is shaped, and therefore peeled and cored, rather like an apple, although the quince is harder, with a knobby, uneven surface, so be especially careful with the knife.

butterscotch cream quince pie

Crumb Crust for a 9-inch pie shell, made with gingersnaps (page 32)

POACHED QUINCES

2½ cups water

1½ cups sugar

¼ teaspoon ground cinnamon

⅛ teaspoon ground cloves

Half a lemon, thinly sliced

3 quinces, about 1¼ pounds

1½ cups heavy (whipping) cream

2 tablespoons sugar

Butterscotch Sauce (page 40)

Preheat the oven to 325°F. Form and bake the crumb crust as directed in the recipe. Cool completely before filling.

To poach the quinces, combine the water, sugar, cinnamon, cloves, and lemon in a large saucepan. Bring to a boil over high heat and stir for a moment until the sugar dissolves. Turn the heat to low, partially cover the pan, and let the poaching liquid simmer gently while you prepare the fruit.

Using a vegetable peeler, peel the skin from each quince. Use a small, sharp knife where necessary to get to any spots the peeler won't reach. Cut each quince in half and dig out the core; be careful, because the flesh is firm and sometimes hard to cut. Cut each half into 4 wedges and drop them into the poaching liquid. Increase the heat so the liquid returns to a boil, then reduce the heat to low and simmer, partially covered, for about 20 minutes, or until the slices are tender when pierced with the point of a sharp knife. Raise the heat a little if necessary to keep the liquid at a simmer. Remove from the heat and let the quinces cool completely in their liquid. Once cooled, the quinces may sit in their liquid, refrigerated, for a day or two.

To prepare the filling, drain the quinces well, discarding the poaching liquid, and pat the slices dry with paper towels. Set aside.

Combine the cream and sugar in a deep, narrow bowl or quart-size measuring cup and, using a hand-held beater or electric mixer, beat until the cream stands in stiff peaks.

Makes one 9-inch pie

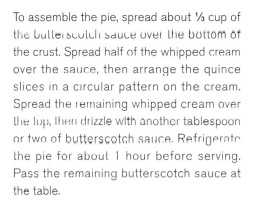

To assemble the pie, spread about ⅓ cup of the butterscotch sauce over the bottom of the crust. Spread half of the whipped cream over the sauce, then arrange the quince slices in a circular pattern on the cream. Spread the remaining whipped cream over the top, then drizzle with another tablespoon or two of butterscotch sauce. Refrigerate the pie for about 1 hour before serving. Pass the remaining butterscotch sauce at the table.

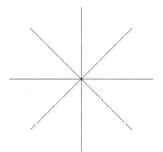

Making a pie of fresh strawberries while retaining the berries' flavor and aroma can be difficult. A pie made of whole fresh berries does not cut easily or neatly, and a pie of long-cooked berries will lack the essence of freshness that made the berries special to start with. The following method, which involves mashing, sweetening, and briefly cooking half the berries and then adding the remaining berries in slices (or whole, if they are small), is the best technique I have found for making a pie that keeps a fresh berry flavor and cuts neatly.

fresh strawberry pie

Basic All-American Pie Dough for a 9-inch pie shell (page 20)

1 ³/₄ to 2 pounds fresh strawberries, 6 to 8 cups, depending on berry size

¹/₄ cup cornstarch

³/₄ cup sugar

Pinch of salt

2 tablespoons fresh lemon juice

Whipped Cream (page 39)

Preheat the oven to 425°F. Roll out the dough and fit it into a 9-inch pie pan. Trim and flute the edges, then bake the pie shell fully, following the instructions on page 22. Cool completely before filling.

Dump the berries into a colander and rinse them. Drain well, shaking to remove excess water, then remove the stems. Pick out about 1 cup of whole berries and reserve for garnish. Cut half of the remaining berries into thick slices (or leave them whole if they are small) and set aside.

Put the remaining whole berries in a medium saucepan and crush them with a potato masher. Add the cornstarch, sugar, and salt and stir until the cornstarch has dissolved completely. Cook over medium heat, stirring almost constantly, until the mixture boils and thickens. Reduce the heat and cook gently for about 1 minute. Remove from the heat and stir in the lemon juice, then cool for 20 to 30 minutes, stirring 2 or 3 times, until just faintly warm.

Stir in the sliced strawberries. Pour the mixture into the pie shell, and refrigerate for 2 to 3 hours, until the filling is softly set.

Before serving, prepare the whipped cream and spread it over the pie. Garnish with the whole berries.

Makes one 9-inch pie

cream pies

Cream pies and custard pies are similar in that they are based on milk and eggs, but for the cook, cream pies are easier and more forgiving. That's because their fillings are thickened with cornstarch and cooked on the stovetop, rather than in the oven, and poured into a fully baked pie shell. While delicate custards are thickened with eggs alone and lose their silky texture if overbaked, the addition of starch to a cream pie makes a filling that stands up to boiling temperatures without harm. Like custard pies, cream pies are at their best when freshly made.

Some cream and custard fillings are made with plain milk, others with evaporated milk—milk from which some of the water has been removed. Evaporated milk is sold in cans and is not refrigerated. It is lower in fat than heavy cream but has about the same consistency. Once a staple in cooking and baking, it has a rich, vaguely caramely flavor that is right in sync with old-fashioned cream and custard pies. Although its use has faded, I continue to think that in some fillings, its once-familiar taste blends well with the other ingredients.

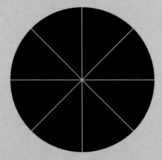

If you are in a hurry and can't face making a full-dress pie, keep in mind that any cream filling also makes a good, old-fashioned pudding, served on its own in bowls or glasses.

For storage, refrigerate any cream pie, or any milk- or egg-based filling or any pie with a cream or meringue topping.

A popular San Francisco Bay Area restaurant had a menu filled with familiar, old-fashioned dishes, including a butterscotch pudding, served in sundae glasses and finished with whipped cream, that butterscotch fans swooned over. Butter and brown sugar are the flavors generally paired to make butterscotch, but this pudding had a depth that seemed almost unachievable through those ingredients alone. The flavor secret was butterscotch chips; there is no other way to attain that flavor. Based on that memory, here is a butterscotch pie of my own.

butterscotch cream pie

Basic All-American Pie Dough for a 9-inch pie shell (page 20)

1 cup heavy (whipping) cream

1 cup milk

2 tablespoons cornstarch

1/4 teaspoon salt

4 egg yolks

2 cups (one 12-ounce bag) butterscotch morsels

1/4 cup (1/2 stick) unsalted butter

1 teaspoon vanilla extract

Meringue Topping (page 38)

Preheat the oven to 425°F. Roll out the dough and fit it into a 9-inch pie pan. Trim and flute the edges, then bake the pie shell fully, following the instructions on page 22. Cool completely before filling.

Combine the cream, milk, cornstarch, and salt in a medium, heavy-bottomed saucepan and whisk together to dissolve the cornstarch. Cook over moderate heat, whisking almost constantly, until the mixture thickens and boils, then reduce the heat and cook, whisking constantly, for 2 minutes more. Remove from the heat and whisk in the egg yolks, then return to the heat and cook about 2 minutes longer, whisking all the while. Add the butterscotch morsels and stir just until they are melted. Remove from the heat, add the butter and vanilla, and stir until blended and smooth. Set aside to cool for about 20 minutes, stirring once or twice, then spread evenly in the pie crust.

Preheat the broiler and position a rack so the top of the pie will be about 4 inches from the heat. Prepare the meringue topping as directed, then gently spread it over the butterscotch filling (which may still be warm), making sure it touches the edge of the crust all around. Broil for 1 or 2 minutes, until the peaks are browned. Cool before serving.

Makes one 9-inch pie

Fresh pineapple, sweetened and then simmered until tender, indeed makes a rich-tasting pie filling. But since the whole fruit can be unwieldy to handle, I recommend using an already trimmed fresh pineapple or fresh pineapple chunks; either or both can be found in most supermarket produce departments. In a pinch, canned pineapple chunks, well drained, are okay, but their flavor is not quite as pure.

pineapple cream pie

Basic All-American Pie Dough for a 9-inch pie shell (page 20)

2 cups fresh pineapple chunks

1 cup sugar

5 tablespoons cornstarch

1/4 teaspoon salt

2 1/4 cups milk

4 egg yolks

1/4 cup (1/2 stick) unsalted butter, at room temperature

1 teaspoon vanilla extract

Meringue Topping (page 38)

Preheat the oven to 425°F. Roll out the dough and fit it into a 9-inch pie pan. Trim and flute the edges, then bake the pie shell fully, following the instructions on page 22. Cool completely before filling.

To prepare the pineapple, combine it with 1/2 cup of the sugar in a medium saucepan. Bring to a boil over moderate heat, stirring frequently, then reduce the heat and simmer, covered, for about 10 minutes, or until the fruit is very tender. Set aside, uncovered, to cool for about 30 minutes, then mash coarsely; a hand-held immersion blender or an old-fashioned potato masher can be used for this. Set aside.

Combine the remaining 1/2 cup sugar, cornstarch, and salt in a large saucepan and whisk together until evenly blended. Pour in the milk and whisk until smooth. Cook over moderate heat, whisking almost constantly, until the mixture boils. Cook for 2 minutes, then whisk in the egg yolks. When the mixture returns to a boil, reduce the heat to low and cook, whisking or stirring constantly, for 2 minutes more. Stir in the reserved pineapple mixture and cook for 1 more minute. Remove from the heat, add the butter and vanilla, and stir until smooth. Set aside to cool for about 20 minutes, stirring once or twice, then spread evenly in the pie shell.

Preheat the broiler. Prepare the meringue topping as directed and spread it over the pie filling (which may still be warm), making sure it touches the edges of the crust all around. Broil for 1 to 2 minutes, until the tips of the peaks of the meringue are browned. Cool before serving.

Makes one 9-inch pie

Does anyone remember butter brickle, the toasty, buttery, nutty candy bits that give crunch and flavor to butter brickle ice cream? It is easy to make at home, and its texture is a perfect go-along to the soft banana slices, smooth filling, and cream topping in this old-fashioned pie.

butter brickle banana cream pie

Basic All-American Pie Dough for a 9-inch pie shell (page 20)

BUTTER BRICKLE

½ cup sugar

5 tablespoons unsalted butter

½ cup sliced or slivered almonds

FILLING

½ cup sugar

¼ cup cornstarch

¼ teaspoon salt

2¼ cups milk

3 egg yolks

3 tablespoons unsalted butter

1 teaspoon vanilla extract

2 large, ripe bananas

Whipped Cream (page 39)

Preheat the oven to 425°F. Roll out the dough and fit it into a 9-inch pie pan. Trim and flute the edges, then bake the pie shell fully, following the instructions on page 22. Cool completely before filling.

To make the butter brickle, line a shallow baking pan with foil. Combine the sugar, butter, and almonds in a large skillet. Place over medium-high heat and cook, stirring almost constantly, until the bubbling mixture turns golden brown, about 5 minutes. Pour into the foil-lined pan and cool completely; it will harden as it cools. Break the butter brickle into pieces and chop coarsely in a food processor. Set aside.

To make the filling, in a medium, heavy-bottomed saucepan whisk together the sugar, cornstarch, and salt. Pour in the milk and whisk until smooth. Place over moderate heat and cook, whisking almost constantly, until the mixture boils. Cook, whisking con-

stantly, for about 2 minutes, then whisk in the egg yolks. Bring the mixture back to a boil, reduce the heat, and cook for 1 minute more. Remove from the heat and stir in the butter and vanilla. Set aside to cool for about 20 minutes, stirring 2 or 3 times.

To assemble the pie, spread about ½ cup of the chopped butter brickle in the baked pie shell. Peel the bananas and slice them about ¼ inch thick, placing the slices over the butter brickle as you work. Cover the bananas with the filling and cool to room temperature. Sprinkle the filling with another ½ cup of the butter brickle.

Prepare the whipped cream and spread it over the pie. Sprinkle with the remaining butter brickle. Refrigerate until ready to serve. This pie is particularly good served within a couple of hours. If you need to wait longer, the brickle will gradually soften, but it will not lose its flavor.

Makes one 9-inch pie

If you are looking for a special-occasion pie, this one fills the bill. I think few flavor combinations are better together than coconut, macadamia nuts, and cream. If you toast the coconut and make the filling a day ahead, this pie will go together much faster. Nothing tops it better than a spoonful of rum-flavored whipped cream.

coconut macadamia cream pie

Basic All-American Pie Dough for a 9-inch pie shell (page 20)

COCONUT MACADAMIA LAYER

5 tablespoons unsalted butter

½ cup sugar

¼ cup heavy (whipping) cream

¾ cup macadamia nuts, coarsely chopped

½ cup shredded coconut, toasted (see Note, page 35)

Pinch of salt

2 tablespoons rum

COCONUT CREAM LAYER

¼ cup sugar

2 tablespoons cornstarch

¼ teaspoon salt

1½ cups milk, heated to a simmer

2 egg yolks

2 tablespoons unsalted butter

1 teaspoon vanilla

¾ cup shredded coconut, toasted (see Note, page 35)

Preheat the oven to 425°F. Roll out the pie dough and fit it into a 9-inch pie pan. Trim and flute the edges (see page 22).

To make the coconut macadamia layer, in a medium, heavy-bottomed saucepan, combine the butter and sugar. Place over moderate heat and stir frequently until the butter melts and the mixture begins to boil. Boil, stirring constantly, until the mixture looks thick and creamy, about 2 minutes. Remove from the heat and stir in the cream, nuts, coconut, and salt. Return to the heat and bring the mixture back to a boil, stirring frequently. Remove from the heat and stir in the rum. Pour the mixture into the pie shell.

Bake for 10 minutes, then reduce the heat to 350°F and bake for 12 to 15 minutes longer, until golden brown and bubbling. Cool completely.

To make the coconut cream layer, in a medium saucepan, whisk together the sugar, cornstarch, and salt. Pour the hot milk into the sugar mixture, whisking constantly. Cook over moderate heat, whisking almost constantly, until the mixture boils and thickens slightly, 7 to 10 minutes. Add the egg yolks and continue to cook, whisking constantly, for about 2 minutes longer. Remove from the heat and pour the mixture into a bowl, then stir in the butter and vanilla. Cool to room temperature, stirring occasionally. Stir ½ cup of the coconut into the mixture, then cover and refrigerate until needed.

To assemble the pie, spread the coconut cream evenly over the coconut macadamia layer, then sprinkle with the remaining ¼ cup coconut. The pie will cut more easily if refrigerated for about an hour before serving.

Makes one 9-inch pie

Regardless of pudding memories good, bad, or indifferent, almost everyone likes this pie—a sleek chocolate pudding in a crisp crust. Make a crustless version if you want by pouring the filling into an oiled pie plate. To serve, cut the filling into wedges and have it with chocolate chip cookies, shortbread, or sugar cookies.

chocolate cream pie

Basic All-American Pie Dough for a 9-inch pie shell (page 20)

3 cups milk or evaporated milk

4 ounces (4 squares) unsweetened chocolate, broken into 6 or 8 pieces

¾ cup sugar

¼ cup cornstarch

¼ teaspoon salt

4 egg yolks

¼ cup unsalted (½ stick) unsalted butter

2 teaspoons vanilla extract

Whipped Cream (page 39)

Preheat the oven to 425°F. Roll out the dough and fit it into a 9-inch pie pan. Trim and flute the edges, then bake the pie shell fully, following the instructions on page 22. Cool completely before filling.

Combine the milk and chocolate in a medium saucepan. Place over moderate heat and whisk frequently for about 4 minutes, or until the chocolate is melted. Don't worry if the mixture looks speckled and grainy; it will become smooth later.

In the meantime, combine the sugar, cornstarch, and salt in a medium, heavy-bottomed saucepan and whisk them together until evenly mixed. Continue whisking as you add the chocolate milk in a steady, continuous stream. Add the egg yolks and whisk vigorously until blended.

Cook over moderate heat, whisking almost constantly, for 6 to 8 minutes, until the mixture thickens and comes to a boil. Reduce the heat and boil gently for about 2 minutes, whisking constantly. Remove from the heat, add the butter, and stir until smooth. Press a piece of plastic wrap directly on the surface of the pudding (to keep a skin from forming) and cool for 30 minutes.

Remove the plastic wrap and stir in the vanilla. Pour the pudding into the prepared pie shell and place another sheet of plastic wrap over it. Refrigerate for at least 3 hours, until chilled and firm.

Before serving, prepare the whipped cream and spread it over the pie.

Makes one 9-inch pie

Stirring lemon juice into the cooked filling will not curdle the milk, as you might think it would. To the contrary, it results in a pie with a softly set consistency, creamier and richer than lemon meringue, with a smooth citrus flavor.

lemon cream pie

Crumb Crust for a 9-inch pie shell, made with gingersnaps or graham crackers (page 32)

1 cup sugar

¼ cup cornstarch

¼ teaspoon salt

2½ cups milk or evaporated milk

4 egg yolks

¼ cup (½ stick) unsalted butter, at room temperature

½ cup fresh lemon juice

1 tablespoon grated lemon zest

Whipped Cream (page 39)

Form and bake the crumb crust as directed in the recipe. Cool completely before filling.

Whisk together the sugar, cornstarch, and salt in a medium saucepan. Pour in the milk and whisk until smooth. Cook over moderate heat, whisking almost constantly, until the mixture thickens and comes to a boil. Boil gently for about 2 minutes, whisking constantly. Remove from the heat and add the egg yolks, whisking until blended. Bring the mixture back to a boil, then reduce the heat and cook for 2 minutes more, whisking constantly. Remove from the heat and add the butter, lemon juice, and lemon zest, stirring or whisking until the filling is smooth. Set aside to cool for about 10 minutes, stirring once or twice.

Pour the filling into the prepared crust. Refrigerate for at least 3 hours, until the filling is chilled and firm.

Before serving, prepare the whipped cream and spread it over the pie.

Makes one 9-inch pie

You don't need much skill to make this pie, which is simply melted chocolate blended with whipped cream and scooped into either a crumb or coconut crust. Folding the cream and chocolate together just partially gives the filling a mottled, tweedy appearance, and the finished pie looks like a lot more work than it really is. Given the amounts of chocolate and cream, this really has quite a light texture.

chocolate tweed pie

Crumb Crust for a 9-inch pie shell, made with chocolate wafers (page 32), or Toasted Coconut Crust for a 9-inch pie shell (page 34)

2 cups (12 ounces) semisweet chocolate morsels

1¼ cups heavy (whipping) cream

2 teaspoons vanilla extract

Pinch of salt

Whipped Cream (page 39), for topping

Form and bake the crust as directed in the recipe. Cool completely before filling.

Fill a large saucepan about halfway with water, then place over moderate heat. Pour the chocolate morsels into a glass or metal bowl that can be set comfortably inside the rim of the saucepan. When the water is quite hot, but not simmering, set the bowl of chocolate in it. Stir constantly for 2 to 3 minutes, until the chocolate is mostly melted. Remove the bowl from the water and continue stirring until the chocolate is smooth. Set aside for about 15 minutes, stirring 2 or 3 times, until the chocolate feels cool, not warm, to your finger, but is still soft and workable.

In a medium bowl, whip the cream with the vanilla and salt until it forms soft peaks. Pour the chocolate mixture over the cream and, with a rubber spatula or a big wooden spoon, fold them together quickly but gently for a few seconds, so there are streaks of dark and white and flecks of chocolate. Pour the mixture into the prepared crust and spread it evenly. Chill for at least 2 hours.

Before serving, prepare the whipped cream for the topping and spread it over the pie.

Makes one 9-inch pie

custard pies

Custard pies, with their foundation of eggs, milk, sugar, and flavorings, can be delicate and sleek. Because they depend solely on eggs for thickening, you need to keep an eye on them in the oven and watch the baking time, remembering that the center of the pie will continue to firm up as the pie cools. A custard that is overbaked can be a little grainy and watery, yet is still eminently edible. Just bake your next pie a little less.

Unfortunately, custard pies often get a bad rap for having a soggy bottom crust. There are all sorts of suggested remedies for preventing this, from prebaking the pie shell until it is partially crisp before adding the filling, to warming the filling on the stovetop before pouring it into the pie shell, sprinkling the pie shell with sugar, or brushing the pie shell with egg white or melted jelly. For the home cook, all these ideas simply add another step to an already daunting process. Because my goal is to get you to bake pies, not scare you away from them, I'll let you in on my simple technique for minimizing the soggy crust syndrome: Bake pies in a glass pie plate, in a fully preheated oven, and serve them within a few hours. It isn't a perfect solution, but it's a manageable one.

Once the filling has set and reached room temperature, try to serve custard pies as soon as possible. These are, as one pie-baking friend used to say, real "right now pies." But if you have leftovers, remember that any pie with a milk- or egg-based filling should be refrigerated for storage.

Incredible as it sounds, in the past,
it was not uncommon to christen foods, particularly desserts, after political figures.
Named for the 10th president of the United States, John Tyler of Virginia, this pie has
its heritage in the South. Though the ingredients are simple, the pie has a caramel-like
flavor and a smooth texture that combine to give it a soothing quality. It is as suitable
for breakfast as it is after a good meal.

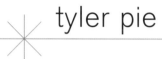

tyler pie

Basic All-American Pie Dough for a 9-inch
pie shell (page 20)

½ cup (1 stick) unsalted butter

1½ cups brown sugar

²/₃ cup heavy (whipping) cream

¼ teaspoon salt

2 teaspoons vanilla extract

3 eggs, beaten

Preheat the oven to 375°F. Roll out the
dough and fit it into a 9-inch glass pie pan,
then trim and flute the edges (see page 22).

Put the butter and the brown sugar in a
medium, heavy-bottomed saucepan and
place over medium-high heat. As the butter
melts, stir or whisk to combine it with the
sugar. Once the mixture is smoothly
blended and beginning to bubble, cook it for
about 2 minutes longer, whisking constantly.
Remove from the heat and add the cream,
then whisk until smooth. Add the salt, vanilla,
and eggs and whisk until evenly blended.

Pour the mixture into the prepared pie shell.
Bake for about 35 minutes, until the filling
quivers slightly when the pan is jiggled, and
the surface is puffy and wavy (once out of the
oven, it will flatten). Cool for at least an hour,
then serve warm or at room temperature.

Makes one 9-inch pie

You might read this recipe and think it's coconut cream pie, but it's not. It is a sweet and candylike pie with a deep coconut flavor, and it goes together in a snap.

coconut custard pie

Basic All-American Pie Dough for a 9-inch pie shell (page 20)

1 cup shredded coconut

3 tablespoons unsalted butter, melted

⅓ cup sugar

3 eggs, at room temperature

1 cup light corn syrup

2 teaspoons vanilla extract

⅓ cup heavy (whipping) cream or evaporated milk

Preheat the oven to 375°F. Roll out the pie dough and fit it into a 9-inch glass pie pan. Trim and flute the edges (see page 22). Spread the coconut over the bottom of the pie shell and set aside.

Combine the melted butter and sugar in a large bowl and whisk until blended. Add the eggs and beat until evenly mixed, then add the corn syrup, vanilla, and cream and whisk until the mixture is smooth. Pour the filling into the pie shell, over the coconut.

Bake for 40 to 50 minutes, until the filling is golden brown and puffy (it will sink as it cools) and trembles slightly if the pan is jiggled. Serve warm or at room temperature.

Makes one 9-inch pie

What could be better with maple syrup than the flavors of butter and cream? Omit the meringue if you want, and instead serve the pie with additional cream, whipped but not sweetened.

maple spice pie

Basic All-American Pie Dough for a 9-inch pie shell (page 20)

¼ cup all-purpose flour

2 tablespoons sugar

¼ teaspoon ground nutmeg

¼ teaspoon ground cinnamon

¼ teaspoon salt

½ cup (1 stick) unsalted butter, at room temperature

4 egg yolks

1¼ cups pure maple syrup

1 cup heavy (whipping) cream

Meringue Topping (page 38)

Preheat the oven to 450°F. Roll out the dough and fit it into a 9-inch glass pie pan, then trim and flute the edges (see page 22).

Combine the flour, sugar, nutmeg, cinnamon, and salt and sift them together, or shake them through a strainer, onto a sheet of waxed paper. Set aside.

Put the butter in a large bowl and, using a big wooden spoon or a hand-held electric mixer, beat for a moment, until it is smooth and creamy. Add the flour mixture and beat again until evenly mixed. Add the egg yolks and beat until incorporated, then whisk in the maple syrup. Add the cream and stir or whisk until blended and smooth. Pour into the prepared pie shell.

Bake for 10 minutes, then reduce the heat to 325°F and continue baking for 40 minutes longer, or until a knife inserted slightly off-center comes out clean. Remove the pie and set aside to cool for about 20 minutes.

In the meantime, prepare the meringue as directed. Preheat the broiler. Gently spread the meringue evenly over the warm pie, making sure it touches the crust all around. Set under the broiler for a minute or two, until the peaks are brown. Let the pie cool before serving.

Makes one 9-inch pie

A good pecan pie can be made in so many ways. Here, the simple step of browning the butter intensifies the nutty pecan flavor. The best accompaniment for this pie is heavy cream, whipped but not sweetened. If you consider pecan pie a slice of paradise on a plate, you are in good company.

pecan pie

Basic All-American Pie Dough (page 20) or Cornmeal Pie Dough (page 24) for a 9-inch pie shell

6 tablespoons (3/4 stick) unsalted butter

1/2 cup sugar

3 eggs, at room temperature

1 cup light corn syrup

1 teaspoon vanilla extract

1/4 teaspoon salt

1 1/2 cups pecan halves

Preheat the oven to 425°F. Roll out the dough and fit it into a 9-inch glass pie pan, then trim and flute the edges. Set aside.

Put the butter in a small saucepan and place over medium heat. As the butter melts, hold the pan by the handle and swirl it in small circles over the heat. Reduce the heat to low, and continue to swirl the pan frequently for about 4 minutes, or until the butter has browned to about the color of a walnut shell. Do not let it burn. Immediately pour the browned butter into a large bowl. Add the sugar and eggs and whisk until evenly blended. Add the corn syrup, vanilla, and salt and whisk again until smooth. Stir in the pecan halves.

Pour the mixture into the prepared pie shell. The nuts will float to the surface; if they look clumped together in one area, use the tines of a fork to spread them around more evenly.

Bake for 15 minutes, then reduce the heat to 350°F and continue to bake for about 25 minutes longer, or until the filling has puffed and set around the edges but the center still quivers slightly. A sharp knife inserted slightly off-center will come out with a film of cooked—not raw—filling on it. Cool for at least 1 hour, then serve warm or at room temperature.

Makes one 9-inch pie

The unorthodox system of cooking the filling on top of the stove and then pouring it into a fully baked, crisp pie shell alleviates the tendency for the crust to be damp under the pumpkin filling. I wish I could take full credit for it, but I can't: It is inspired by a winning recipe from a contest sponsored by the Borden Company way back in 1931. Apparently, cooks are always looking to improve on a classic. The broiled topping, crisp and crunchy over the smooth pumpkin filling, is optional, but it elevates this pie to new heights.

different pumpkin pie

Basic All-American Pie Dough for a 9-inch pie shell (page 20)

PUMPKIN FILLING

1½ cups evaporated milk

1 tablespoon (about 1¼ envelopes) unflavored gelatin

1 teaspoon ground cinnamon

½ teaspoon ground ginger

½ teaspoon ground cloves

¼ teaspoon salt

3 eggs

¾ cup sugar

2 cups pumpkin purée

TOPPING

1 cup finely chopped walnuts

⅔ cup brown sugar

Pinch of salt

3 tablespoons unsalted butter, melted

Preheat the oven to 425°F. Roll out the dough and fit it into a 9-inch pie pan. Trim and flute the edges, then bake the pie shell fully, following the instructions on page 22. Cool completely before filling.

To make the filling, whisk together the evaporated milk and gelatin in a medium, heavy-bottomed saucepan. Let stand for a few minutes to soften the gelatin. Add the cinnamon, ginger, cloves, and salt and whisk until blended. Add the eggs and sugar and whisk again until blended and smooth. Cook over moderate heat, whisking almost constantly, for 7 to 10 minutes, until the mixture thickens slightly and you see wisps of steam rising, but do not let it boil. Remove from the heat and add the pumpkin, then whisk until completely smooth. Pour the filling into the prepared pie shell and refrigerate for at least 4 hours, or overnight if you prefer. The filling will become firm as it cools.

To make the topping, preheat the broiler and position a rack so that the surface of the pie will be about 4 inches from the heat. Combine the walnuts, brown sugar, salt, and butter in a small bowl and stir briskly with a fork until evenly mixed. Spread over the surface of the cooled pie. Broil for about 2 minutes, or until the topping is lightly browned and bubbly. Watch the pie like a hawk for this short time, and rotate it once or twice as necessary so the topping browns evenly. Let cool before serving. The topping may be broiled several hours ahead; although it will lose a little of its crunch, it will still be very good.

Makes one 9-inch pie

A crumbly top covers a layer of moist cake over a thin, caramel like base in this pie. Also known by the less appealing—and undeserved—name of gravel pie, it will win you over with its spicy flavor, reminiscent of an old-fashioned coffee cake.

crumb pie

Basic All-American Pie Dough for a 9-inch pie shell (page 20)

CRUMB TOPPING

1 1/4 cups all-purpose flour

1/4 cup sugar

1/2 teaspoon ground cinnamon

1/2 teaspoon ground nutmeg

1/4 teaspoon salt

6 tablespoons (3/4 stick) unsalted butter, at room temperature

FILLING

2/3 cup boiling water

1 cup brown sugar

1/2 teaspoon baking soda

2 eggs

Preheat the oven to 450°F. Roll out the dough and fit it into a 9-inch glass pie pan, then trim and flute the edges (see page 22).

To make the topping, in a large bowl stir together the flour, sugar, cinnamon, nutmeg, and salt, using a whisk or fork. Cut the butter into several pieces and drop them into the bowl. Using your fingertips or a pastry blender, blend the butter into the flour until there are no visible pieces of butter and the mixture resembles coarse, dry crumbs. Set aside.

To make the filling, in a medium bowl, whisk together the boiling water and brown sugar. Add the baking soda and whisk until you don't see any small lumps. Add the eggs and whisk until they are completely incorporated, with no drifts of unblended white or yolk. The mixture will be quite thin. Pour into the prepared pie shell, and sprinkle evenly with the topping.

Bake for 10 minutes, then reduce the heat to 350°F and bake for 25 to 30 minutes longer. As the pie bakes it will puff dramatically and the crumb surface will crack in several places; it is done when a knife inserted slightly off-center, into one of the cracks, comes out clean, with no runny, raw filling on it. Cool for at least 1 hour before serving. The filling will sink slightly as it cools.

Makes one 9-inch pie

If you think this is just another nut pie, you are wrong—it is quite surprising what the blend of chocolate and walnuts does for the rich filling. It is at once pudding-like and vaguely chewy, and the chocolate tempers the sweetness often associated with nut pies. Note that the walnuts should be left in large, recognizable pieces.

chocolate walnut pie

Basic All-American Pie Dough for a 9-inch pie shell (page 20)

3 eggs, at room temperature

1 cup light corn syrup

½ cup sugar

2 teaspoons vanilla extract

¼ teaspoon salt

¼ cup (½ stick) unsalted butter, melted

2 ounces (2 squares) unsweetened chocolate, melted

1¾ cups walnut halves and pieces

Preheat the oven to 425°F. Roll out the dough and fit it into a 9-inch glass pie pan, then trim and flute the edges (see page 22). Set aside.

In a large bowl, beat the eggs until the yolks and whites are blended. Add the corn syrup, sugar, vanilla, salt, and butter, and beat until evenly mixed. Add the chocolate and continue beating until smooth. Stir in the walnuts. Pour the mixture into the prepared pie shell. The walnuts will rise to the suface; if they clump together, redistribute them more evenly with the tines of a fork.

Bake for 15 minutes, then reduce the heat to 350°F and continue baking for about 25 minutes longer, or until the filling has puffed slightly and has set around the edges but the center is still slightly trembly (it will become firm as it cools). Cool for at least 1 hour, then serve warm or at room temperature.

Makes one 9-inch pie

This recipe is not as complicated as it might sound. It is really quite simple to slip the cooked custard into the baked shell, thus producing that rare union of delicate custard filling and fully crisp crust. This pie has a comforting, soothing quality, and the maple syrup isn't masked by other flavors.

maple nutmeg custard pie

Basic All-American Pie Dough for a 9-inch pie shell (page 20)

MAPLE CUSTARD FILLING

1 cup heavy (whipping) cream

1 cup maple syrup

½ cup milk

3 eggs

3 egg yolks

1 teaspoon ground nutmeg

Pinch of salt

TOPPING

1 cup heavy (whipping) cream

1 tablespoon nonfat dry milk

2 tablespoons maple syrup

Preheat the oven to 425°F. Roll out the dough and fit it into a 9-inch pie pan, then trim and flute the edges. Bake the pie shell fully, following the instructions on page 22. Cool completely before filling.

Reduce the oven heat to 350°F. Coat another 9-inch pie pan, the same size and shape as the first one, generously with non-stick cooking spray. Have a large baking dish available that the second pie pan will fit into. Bring a kettle of water to a simmer.

To make the maple custard, combine the cream, maple syrup, and milk in a medium saucepan and place over moderate heat. Stir occasionally until the mixture is quite hot and you see wisps of steam rising, but do not let it boil.

Meanwhile, combine the eggs, egg yolks, nutmeg, and salt in a large bowl and whisk briskly to blend. Continue whisking as you pour in the hot syrup mixture. Pour into the prepared pie pan (the one without the crust), then set the pie pan in the large baking dish. Pour about ½ inch of simmering water into the outer baking dish.

Place in the oven and bake for 35 to 40 minutes, or until the custard is set around the edges but the center remains slightly trembly. A knife inserted slightly off-center should come out almost clean, or with traces of baked—not raw—custard on it. Carefully lift the pie pan from the water and set it aside on a rack to cool for at least 1 hour, or until the bottom of the pan is barely warm to your hand.

Makes one 9-inch pie

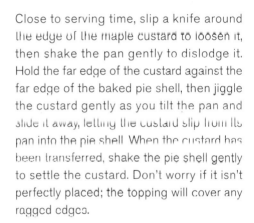

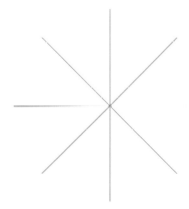

Close to serving time, slip a knife around the edge of the maple custard to loosen it, then shake the pan gently to dislodge it. Hold the far edge of the custard against the far edge of the baked pie shell, then jiggle the custard gently as you tilt the pan and slide it away, letting the custard slip from its pan into the pie shell. When the custard has been transferred, shake the pie shell gently to settle the custard. Don't worry if it isn't perfectly placed; the topping will cover any ragged edges.

To make the topping, whip the cream with the dry milk until it stands in stiff peaks. Add the maple syrup and whip until blended. Spread over the top of the pie.

A thin layer of lime custard under a billowy, sweet meringue makes this pie a real treat. The pronounced lime flavor gives it a refreshing quality and lends the illusion of lightness. Given the richness of the ingredients, however, it is anything but.

fresh lime pie

Crumb Crust for a 9-inch pie shell, made with gingersnaps or graham crackers (page 32)

5 egg yolks

2 teaspoons cornstarch

⅔ cup fresh lime juice

¼ teaspoon salt

1 tablespoon grated lime zest

1¼ cups sugar

1 tablespoon unsalted butter

Meringue Topping (page 38)

Form and bake the crumb crust as directed in the recipe.

Put the egg yolks and cornstarch in a medium, heavy-bottomed saucepan and whisk together briskly for about 1 minute. Add the lime juice, salt, zest, and sugar and whisk until the ingredients are blended and smooth.

Cook over moderate heat, whisking constantly and taking care to reach all over the bottom of the pan as you whisk, for 8 to 10 minutes, or until the mixture thickens slightly and comes to a boil. As it cooks, it will increase somewhat in volume and the surface will look foamy; this will subside as the mixture boils. Remove from the heat, add the butter, and continue whisking, off the heat, for about 1 minute. Set aside to cool for about 20 minutes, stirring once or twice.

Pour the lime custard into the prepared crust, spreading it evenly.

Prepare the meringue as directed. Preheat the broiler and adjust a rack so the pie will be about 4 inches from the heat. Gently spread the meringue over the pie, making sure it touches the edge of the crust all around. Set it under the broiler for a minute or two, until the peaks are brown. Let the pie cool before serving.

Makes one 9-inch pie

Though fresh is usually best in baking, dried fruit, with some doctoring, can make a very good pie as well. Dried apricots would work equally well in this pie of tangy buttermilk custard over a sweet layer of fruit purée.

peach buttermilk pie

1 ¾ cups dried peaches, about 6 ounces

1 cup water

1 ¼ cups sugar

Basic All-American Pie Dough for a 9-inch pie shell (page 20)

2 tablespoons all-purpose flour

¼ teaspoon salt

3 eggs

1 ½ cups buttermilk

Using a sharp knife or kitchen scissors, cut the peaches into pieces about ½ inch square, more or less, dropping them into a medium saucepan as you work. Add the water and ½ cup of the sugar to the peaches. Place over high heat and bring to a boil, then reduce the heat to low and continue to cook, stirring frequently, for about 20 minutes, until the mixture thickens and the fruit is soft. Using a potato masher or a hand-held beater, mash the fruit until it becomes a coarse purée. Set aside to cool for about 20 minutes.

Preheat the oven to 425°F. Roll out the pie dough and fit it into a 9-inch glass pie pan, then trim and flute the edges (see page 22).

Spread 1 cup of the peach mixture in the bottom of the prepared pie shell. Scrape the remaining peach mixture (about ½ cup) into a large bowl. Add the remaining ¾ cup sugar, along with the flour, salt, and eggs. Beat or whisk briskly until evenly blended and you don't see any lumps of flour. Stir in the buttermilk. Pour the buttermilk mixture into the pie shell, over the peach purée.

Bake for 15 minutes, then reduce the heat to 325°F and continue baking for about 30 minutes longer, until the rim of the crust is browned and the custard is set—the edges will be firm and the center will jiggle just slightly when the pie is moved.

Serve warm or at room temperature.

Makes one 9-inch pie

Here is a pie reminiscent of cheesecake, but easier to make because you don't need a special pan. It is studded with plump, rum-soaked raisins and spread with a tangy sour cream topping that is a perfect counterpart to the rich cream cheese filling. Rum and raisins go together like old friends, so combine them and set aside to soak overnight if you think about it.

rum raisin cream cheese pie

1/3 cup rum

1 cup raisins

Basic All-American Pie Dough for a 9-inch pie shell (page 20)

12 ounces (1½ cups) cream cheese, at room temperature

2/3 cup sugar

¼ teaspoon salt

2 eggs

2/3 cup heavy (whipping) cream

1 teaspoon vanilla extract

SOUR CREAM TOPPING

1 cup sour cream

3 tablespoons sugar

Pour the rum into a small saucepan and bring it just to a simmer over moderate heat—this takes only a moment; do not let it boil. Add the raisins, cover the pan, and set aside off the heat for at least 1 hour. (The raisins may soak in the rum overnight if you wish.)

Preheat the oven to 425°F. Roll out the dough and fit it into a 9-inch glass pie pan, then trim and flute the edges (see page 22). Set aside.

In a large bowl, using a hand-held electric mixer or a big wooden spoon, beat the cream cheese until it is soft and smooth. Add the sugar and salt and continue beating until blended. Add the eggs and beat until smooth. Stir in the cream and vanilla. Stir in the raisins, along with any rum left from soaking. Pour the mixture into the prepared pie shell.

Bake for 10 minutes, then reduce the heat to 350°F and continue baking for 20 to 25 minutes longer, or until the filling has puffed slightly and has set around the edges. The center should remain slightly soft; it will become firm as it cools. Let the pie cool for 1 hour. Don't worry if the surface cracks—the topping will cover any blemishes.

To make the topping, stir together the sour cream and sugar until the sugar dissolves. Spread over the pie and refrigerate for several hours before serving.

Makes one 9-inch pie

There are many versions of this time-honored pie, generally made with eggs or egg yolks, butter, sugar, cornmeal, and a little vinegar, which results in a surprising, yet mild, cheesy flavor. There are also varying explanations regarding the name. My favorite is that the cooks who made it, with simple ingredients that would have been in any well-stocked larder of the time, said it was "jes' pie." In other words, it's nothing fancy, but it's quick to make and it tastes good.

 # chess pie

Basic All-American Pie Dough (page 20) or Cornmeal Pie Dough (page 24) for a 9-inch pie shell

TOPPING

½ cup brown sugar

1 tablespoon chilled unsalted butter

½ teaspoon ground cinnamon

FILLING

4 eggs, at room temperature

1 cup sugar

3 tablespoons cornmeal

1 tablespoon plus 1 teaspoon cider vinegar

¼ teaspoon salt

10 tablespoons (1¼ sticks) unsalted butter, melted

1 teaspoon vanilla extract

Preheat the oven to 350°F. Roll out the dough and fit it into a 9-inch glass pie pan, then trim and flute the edges (see page 22).

To make the topping, combine the sugar, butter, and cinnamon in a small bowl. Using your fingertips, rapidly rub the ingredients together until the butter is evenly blended into the sugar. Set aside.

To make the filling, in a medium bowl combine the eggs, sugar, cornmeal, vinegar, salt, butter, and vanilla and whisk until smooth and blended. Pour into the prepared pie shell.

Bake for about 30 minutes, or until the filling is softly set but the center is still quite trembly. Carefully remove the pie from the oven—remember, the filling is soft and hot—and sprinkle it with the topping. Don't worry about getting it perfectly even. Return to the oven and bake for about 10 minutes longer, or until the filling is more firmly set and the topping has melted.

Serve warm or at room temperature.

Makes one 9-inch pie

There are numerous versions of this apple custard dessert, which harkens back to Colonial times. Although you can make a good Marlborough pie with applesauce (and many recipes do), diced fresh apples, cooked gently in butter and sugar and then lightly spiced and combined with eggs and cream, result in a delicate pie with a flavor and texture that I find far and away better than the others I've tried.

marlborough pie

Basic All-American Pie Dough for a 9-inch pie shell (page 20)

3 Golden Delicious apples, 1 to 1¼ pounds

¼ cup (½ stick) unsalted butter

⅔ cup sugar

1 tablespoon fresh lemon juice

¼ teaspoon ground cinnamon

¼ teaspoon ground nutmeg

1 cup heavy (whipping) cream

3 eggs

¼ teaspoon salt

Preheat the oven to 350°F. Roll out the dough and fit it into a 9-inch glass pie pan, then trim and flute the edges (see page 22).

Peel, halve, and core the apples. Cut each half into 4 pieces, then cut the pieces crosswise into ½-inch chunks. Set aside. In a large skillet over medium-high heat, melt the butter and sugar together, stirring frequently. Add the apples and stir to coat with the sugar mixture. The apples will quickly exude a lot of juice. Continue cooking over moderate heat, stirring frequently, for 10 to 15 minutes, until the juices have mostly evaporated and the apples are fairly tender; the bubbling liquid remaining in the skillet will have a thick, syrupy consistency. Remove from the heat and stir in the lemon juice, cinnamon, and nutmeg. Set aside to cool for about 10 minutes.

In a medium bowl, whisk together the cream, eggs, and salt until evenly blended. Add the apples, making sure to include any of the syrupy liquid remaining in the skillet. Stir gently but thoroughly to combine the apples and custard. Pour into the prepared pie shell.

Bake for 45 to 50 minutes, until the filling has puffed around the edges and browned lightly; the center should be softly set, and a knife inserted into it will come out with a film of cooked, but not raw, filling on it. Cool for at least 1 hour before serving. The filling will sink as it cools.

Makes one 9-inch pie

It's nice to have a few good and simple desserts in any collection, and if you have a homemade pie shell in the freezer, or you start with a store-bought crust, this pie can be ready for the oven in minutes. You can do amazing things with a jar of caramel or butterscotch sauce (they are interchangeable), as this rich, candylike pie shows, or you can make an equally tasty chocolate version, starting with a jar of fudge sauce.

caramel custard pie

Basic All-American Pie Dough for a 9-inch pie shell (page 20)

1½ cups (one 12-ounce jar) caramel sauce or butterscotch sauce

⅔ cup heavy (whipping) cream

⅓ cup brown sugar

3 eggs

2 teaspoons vanilla extract

1 cup chopped walnuts or shredded sweetened coconut

Preheat the oven to 350°F. Roll out the dough and fit it into a 9-inch pie pan. Set aside.

If your sauce is quite thick and difficult to scrape from the jar, microwave it for a moment or two to warm it gently and soften it. In a large bowl, combine the caramel sauce, cream, brown sugar, eggs, vanilla, and walnuts and whisk until evenly mixed. Pour into the prepared pie shell.

Bake for 40 to 45 minutes, until the top has browned slightly and the filling has puffed and set around the edges while the center remains somewhat soft and trembly. (A pie made with chocolate fudge sauce can take several minutes longer to bake than one made with caramel sauce.)

Serve warm or at room temperature.

Makes one 9-inch pie

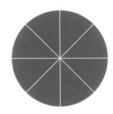

chiffon pies

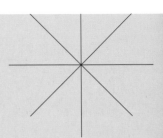

In fashion, chiffon is a light and shimmery fabric. Translated into a pie, the meaning is much the same, for chiffon fillings are nothing more than an egg yolk custard into which beaten egg whites and whipped cream are folded. The resulting pie is at once creamy and rich, with an ethereal taste and texture. Chiffon pies are deceptively light, by virtue of their airiness and slightly trembly nature.

A little gelatin gives stability to these pies and makes the fluffy filling just firm enough to cut neatly. Unflavored gelatin—not be confused with sweetened, fruit-flavored gelatin mixes—is quite simple to work with. Once it has been softened in cold liquid, it dissolves easily into the other ingredients, but you must be careful not to boil it while cooking the custard, or its jelling power will be diminished.

Making a chiffon pie is not difficult, but it does require that you have your wits about you and that you be around to keep an eye on things for a while. Knowing when to remove the custard from the heat, and when it is ready to receive the whipped cream and beaten egg whites, is important. These recipes are detailed enough that if you follow them carefully, you will have success.

Note: Gauging when the cooled, partially set custard is ready to be taken from the refrigerator and folded together with beaten egg whites and/or whipped cream is the only challenging moment in producing a lofty, smooth chiffon pie. A custard that is too cold and stiff will be difficult to fold into the other ingredients. Since exact, to-the minute timing isn't possible to provide considering every variable, I have given visual clues and approximate times in the recipes, and suggest you proceed with whipping the cream and beating the egg whites, using a hand-held electric mixer, 5 to 10 minutes before you anticipate the custard to be properly chilled. After you've made a pie or two, you'll follow your instincts and know what timing works for you.

The flavors of orange and chocolate are very good together. Have you tried pouring a little orange liqueur over chocolate pudding, or adding it to a chocolate mousse recipe? Here a chocolate crumb crust meets an orange chiffon filling. Made without beaten egg whites, this pie is particularly rich, depending as it does solely on whipped cream for lightness. If you like, garnish with grated or shaved semisweet chocolate, and serve with additional whipped cream.

orange chiffon pie

Crumb Crust for a 9-inch pie shell, made with chocolate wafer cookies (page 32)

1 tablespoon (about 1¼ envelopes) unflavored gelatin

¾ cup fresh orange juice

2 tablespoons fresh lemon juice

¾ cup sugar

4 egg yolks

2 tablespoons grated orange zest

¼ teaspoon salt

1 cup milk

¼ cup orange liqueur (optional)

1½ cups heavy (whipping) cream

Form and bake the crumb crust as directed in the recipe. Cool completely before filling.

In a medium, heavy-bottomed saucepan, sprinkle the gelatin over the orange juice and lemon juice. Stir with a fork, and let stand for a few minutes to soften the gelatin. Add the sugar, egg yolks, orange zest, and salt and whisk until blended. Whisk in the milk. Cook over moderate heat, whisking almost constantly. After 3 to 4 minutes, the mixture will become foamy. Cook for 3 to 5 minutes longer, until it has thickened slightly and you see wisps of steam rising; do not allow it to boil. Pour immediately into a large bowl. Refrigerate, whisking about every 10 minutes, until the mixture feels cool and a spoonful of it lifted and dropped back onto the surface leaves a small mound. Depending on the size and depth of your bowl, this will take 1 to 2 hours (longer than most chiffon mixtures). Stir in the orange liqueur, if using.

About 5 to 10 minutes before you anticipate the orange mixture to be ready, in a medium bowl, whip the cream until it forms stiff peaks. Scoop the cream over the orange mixture and, using a rubber spatula, fold the two together quickly yet gently, until there are no drifts of unblended cream. Pour the mixture into the prepared pie crust, mounding it in the center. Chill for several hours before serving.

Makes one 9-inch pie

With a fluffy texture and a pure flavor, this pie is typical of the lofty "mile high" pies that were popular decades ago, when electric mixers were becoming basic equipment in most home kitchens. Electricity rescued the cook from the labor of whipping all those egg whites by hand and gave rise to some of the lightest, airiest pies ever made. See page 137 for a genuine Mile High Strawberry Pie.

116

lemon chiffon pie

Basic All-American Pie Dough (page 20) or Crumb Crust for a 9-inch pie shell, made with gingersnaps (page 32)

1 tablespoon (about 1¼ envelopes) unflavored gelatin

⅓ cup water

1¼ cups sugar

⅔ cup fresh lemon juice

5 egg yolks

2 tablespoons freshly grated lemon zest

5 egg whites

¼ teaspoon salt

If you are using pie dough, preheat the oven to 425°F. Roll out the dough and fit it into a 9-inch pie pan, then trim and flute the edges. Bake the pie shell fully, following the instructions on page 22.

If you are using a crumb crust, form and bake the crust as directed in the recipe. Cool either crust completely before filling.

In a medium size, heavy-bottomed saucepan, sprinkle the gelatin over the water. Let stand for a few minutes to soften the gelatin. Add ¾ cup of the sugar and the lemon juice and whisk until blended. Add the egg yolks and whisk again until smooth. Cook over medium heat, whisking constantly. After 3 to 4 minutes, the mixture will become foamy and will nearly double in volume. After 3 to 5 minutes more cooking, the mixture will thicken slightly and you will see wisps of steam rising. Do not let it boil. Remove from the heat and immediately pour the steaming mixture into a large bowl. Stir in the lemon zest.

Refrigerate, whisking every 7 to 10 minutes, until the mixture has cooled and thickened slightly; it will feel tepid, not chilled, to your finger, and a spoonful of it lifted and dropped back onto the surface will leave a small mound. This will take 40 minutes to 1 hour, depending on the size of the bowl and the depth of the mixture in it. At this point, proceed quickly to the egg whites.

Makes one 9-inch pie

Put the egg whites in a large bowl and add the salt. Beat until the whites stand in very soft peaks (a hand-held electric mixer is useful for this), then gradually add the remaining ½ cup sugar and continue beating until the whites stand in fluffy peaks that droop slightly when the beater is lifted. If you are in doubt, it is better to underbeat than overbeat. Stir a big spoonful of the beaten whites into the lemon mixture, then pour the lemon mixture over the whites and, using a rubber spatula or large wooden spoon, fold together gently until there are no drifts of unblended white. Pile the mixture into the prepared pie crust, mounding it in the center. Refrigerate for several hours before serving.

Chocolate blended with a hefty dose of coffee produces the rich and stimulating taste of mocha. These well-matched flavors give such an illusion of lightness that this pie is a dandy finish to a substantial but simple dinner.

mocha mousse chiffon pie

Crumb Crust for a 9-inch pie shell, made with graham crackers or chocolate wafer cookies (page 32)

1 tablespoon (about 1¼ envelopes) unflavored gelatin

½ cup cold water

1 cup milk

1 tablespoon instant coffee granules

3 ounces (3 squares) unsweetened chocolate, chopped

1 cup sugar

4 egg yolks

¼ teaspoon salt

1 tablespoon vanilla extract

4 egg whites

⅔ cup heavy (whipping) cream

Form and bake the crumb crust as directed in the recipe. Cool completely before filling.

Sprinkle the gelatin over the water in a small bowl and let it stand for a few minutes to soften. Combine the milk, coffee, and chocolate in a medium, heavy-bottomed saucepan and place over moderate heat. Whisk or stir frequently for 4 to 5 minutes, or until the chocolate melts. Remove from the heat and continue to stir for a minute, then add ½ cup of the sugar, egg yolks, and salt, and whisk until blended. Return to moderate heat and cook, whisking constantly, for 4 to 6 minutes, until the mixture thickens slightly and you see wisps of steam rising. Do not let it boil. Remove from the heat and whisk in the softened gelatin. Return to moderate heat and whisk for about 1 minute more to melt the gelatin, but do not let the mixture boil. Immediately pour into a large bowl and stir in the vanilla.

Refrigerate, stirring every 10 minutes, until the mixture is cool and beginning to thicken and hold its shape, 40 minutes to 1 hour.

About 5 minutes before you anticipate the mocha mixture to be ready, beat the egg whites in a large bowl until they form soft peaks. Add the remaining ½ cup sugar and beat until the whites stand in stiff peaks. In a separate, medium bowl, whip the cream until it too stands in soft peaks; you may use the same beaters.

Scoop the whipped cream onto the beaten whites, then pour the chocolate mixture on top. Using a rubber spatula or a large wooden spoon, fold everything together quickly yet gently until you see no drifts of unblended white. Scoop the mixture into the prepared pie crust, mounding it in the center. Refrigerate for several hours before serving.

Makes one 9-inch pie

What has happened to thick, frosty chocolate malts, with a creamy texture and plenty of malt flavor and aroma? They seem to have gone the way of buggy wheels. Thankfully, malted milk powder survives—it's usually found in the cocoa or coffee section of the grocery store—so you can continue to enjoy this time-honored blend of flavors in a billowy chiffon pie.

chocolate malt chiffon pie

Crumb Crust for a 9-inch pie shell, made with graham crackers or chocolate wafer cookies (page 32)

1 envelope (1 scant tablespoon) unflavored gelatin

¼ cup cold water

1¼ cups milk

2 ounces (2 squares) unsweetened chocolate, chopped

¼ teaspoon salt

⅔ cup sugar

3 egg yolks

⅔ cup malted milk powder

2 teaspoons vanilla extract

3 egg whites

1 cup heavy (whipping) cream

Form and bake the crumb crust as directed in the recipe. Cool completely before filling.

Sprinkle the gelatin over the water in a small bowl and set aside for a few minutes to soften.

In the meantime, combine the milk and chocolate in a medium, heavy-bottomed saucepan and place over moderate heat. Cook, stirring or whisking often, for about 5 minutes, until the chocolate melts. Remove from the heat and add the salt, ⅓ cup of the sugar, and egg yolks, and whisk until smooth and blended. Return to moderate heat and cook, whisking constantly, for about 5 minutes, until the mixture thickens slightly. The surface will look foamy and you will see wisps of steam rising; do not let it boil. Add the softened gelatin and continue to whisk for about 30 seconds longer to melt the gelatin.

Remove from the heat and pour into a large bowl. Add the malt powder and vanilla and whisk until smooth. Refrigerate, stirring or whisking every 7 to 10 minutes, until the mixture has cooled but is not thoroughly chilled and has thickened to about the consistency of cooked hot cereal. Depending on the size and shape of the bowl and the depth of the mixture, this will take from 45 minutes to 1 hour.

About 5 minutes before you anticipate the chocolate malt mixture to be ready, prepare the egg whites and whipped cream (a hand-held electric mixer will be useful for beating both). Beat the egg whites in a large bowl until soft peaks form. Add the remaining ⅓ cup sugar and continue beating until the whites stand in stiff, shiny peaks. Whip the cream in a separate, medium bowl until it too stands in soft peaks. You may use the same beaters, and it is not necessary to wash them.

Makes one 9-inch pie

Scoop the whipped cream and egg whites onto the chocolate mixture and, using a rubber spatula or a large wooden spoon, fold everything together, quickly yet gently, until evenly mixed and there are no drifts of unblended white. Pour the mixture into the prepared crust, mounding it in the center. If you wish, swirl the surface with a spoon to make a decorative pattern. Chill for several hours before serving.

Either mangoes or papayas can be used with equal success and good flavor in this pie. Both fruits have a refreshing, cloudlike quality that makes this a good way to say "happily ever after" following a rich or spicy meal.

tropical chiffon pie

Crumb Crust for a 9-inch pie shell, made with gingersnaps or graham crackers (page 32)

2 ripe papayas or mangoes

1 tablespoon (about 1¼ envelopes) unflavored gelatin

¼ cup water

5 egg yolks

3 tablespoons fresh lime juice

⅔ cup sugar

1 tablespoon grated peeled fresh ginger, or 1 teaspoon ground ginger

5 egg whites

¼ teaspoon salt

Form and bake the crumb crust as directed in the recipe. Cool completely before filling.

Peel the mangoes or papayas. If using mangoes, slice the flesh off the pit. If using papayas, halve them, then scrape out and discard the seeds. Purée the fruit in a food processor. You should have about 1½ cups of fruit purée. Set the purée aside.

In a small bowl, sprinkle the gelatin over the water and let it stand for a few minutes.

In a medium, heavy-bottomed saucepan, combine the egg yolks, lime juice, and ⅓ cup of the sugar, and whisk briskly for a moment. Place over moderate heat and cook, whisking constantly, for about 4 minutes, or until the mixture is thick, hot, and foamy. Do not let it boil. Remove from the heat and whisk in the softened gelatin, then return to the heat and whisk constantly for about 30 seconds longer. Pour into a large bowl and stir in the fruit purée and ginger.

Refrigerate, whisking about every 10 minutes, until the mixture has cooled and thickened slightly; it will feel tepid but not chilled to your finger, and a spoonful of it lifted and dropped back onto the surface will leave a small mound. This will take approximately 1 hour, depending on the size of the bowl and the depth of the mixture in it.

About 5 minutes before you anticipate the fruit mixture to be ready, put the egg whites and salt in a large bowl and beat until they stand in soft peaks. Add the remaining sugar and continue to beat until they stand in stiff peaks. Stir a large spoonful of the whites into the purée, then pour the purée over the whites. Fold together until you see no unblended white. Pile into the crust, mounding it in the center. Refrigerate for several hours before serving.

Makes one 9-inch pie

In this pie, a crisp crust is topped with chocolate custard, fluffy rum chiffon, whipped cream, and grated chocolate. After a surge of popularity decades ago, black bottom pie all but disappeared, yet when I eat it, I can't think of any flavors that blend more harmoniously. This is a recipe with several steps, so be sure you have all the ingredients at hand before you start. It takes a bit of time, but the result is worth it.

black bottom pie

Basic All-American Pie Dough for a 9-inch pie shell (page 20)

CUSTARD AND CHIFFON LAYERS

1 tablespoon (about 1¼ envelopes) unflavored gelatin

⅓ cup water

¾ cup sugar

1½ tablespoons cornstarch

¼ teaspoon salt

1½ cups milk

3 egg yolks

1½ ounces (1½ squares) unsweetened chocolate, finely chopped

1 teaspoon vanilla extract

⅓ cup rum

3 egg whites

TOPPING

1 cup heavy (whipping) cream

1½ tablespoons sugar

1 tablespoon grated unsweetened chocolate

Preheat the oven to 425°F. Roll out the dough and fit it into a 9-inch pie pan, then trim and flute the edges. Bake the pie shell fully, following the instructions on page 22. Cool completely before filling.

To make the chocolate custard and rum chiffon layers, in a small cup or bowl, sprinkle the gelatin over the water and let stand for a few minutes to soften. In a medium saucepan, stir together ½ cup of the sugar, the cornstarch, and salt. Pour in the milk in a steady stream, whisking constantly, then add the egg yolks and whisk until evenly blended. Cook over moderate heat, whisking almost constantly, for 6 to 8 minutes, until the mixture boils. Reduce the heat to a simmer and whisk constantly for 2 minutes. Remove from the heat and pour about ¾ cup of the hot mixture over the chopped chocolate in a small bowl. Stir until the chocolate melts, then spread the chocolate mixture in the pie shell and set aside.

Add the softened gelatin to the hot mixture remaining in the pan and whisk to blend. Return to medium-low heat and whisk for about 1 minute, without boiling, to dissolve the gelatin. Pour into a large bowl and stir in the vanilla and rum. Refrigerate, whisking every 10 minutes, until cooled and thickened slightly, 40 to 60 minutes total.

About 5 minutes before you anticipate the rum mixture to be ready, in a large bowl, whip the egg whites until soft peaks form. Add the remaining ¼ cup sugar as you continue to beat until the whites stand in stiff peaks. Pour the rum mixture over the egg whites and fold them together until you see no drifts of unblended white. Spread the rum chiffon over the chocolate, mounding it slightly. Refrigerate for several hours.

To make the topping, before serving, in a medium bowl, whip the cream with the sugar until stiff. Spread over the pie, then sprinkle with the grated chocolate.

Makes one 9-inch pie

If you haven't made a chiffon pie before, this would be a good one to start with. There is no stove-top cooking, and the coconut crust goes together in a trice, even if you've never made a pie shell before. Make the filling with either decaf or regular coffee, depending on whether or not you want a post-dinner caffeine jolt.

coffee chiffon pie

Toasted Coconut Crust for a 9-inch pie (page 34)

1 tablespoon (about 1¼ envelopes) unflavored gelatin

½ cup milk

1½ cups boiling water

¾ cup sugar

1½ tablespoons instant coffee granules

¼ teaspoon salt

¼ cup Kahlúa or other coffee-flavored liqueur, or rum

2 teaspoons vanilla extract

3 egg whites

¾ cup heavy (whipping) cream

Form the coconut crust as directed in the recipe.

Sprinkle the gelatin over the milk in a small bowl and let it stand for a few minutes to soften.

Pour the boiling water (be sure it is really boiling, not just steaming) into a large bowl. Add the softened gelatin, ½ cup of the sugar, the coffee, and the salt. Stir until the gelatin has completely dissolved, 2 to 3 minutes. Stir in the Kahlúa and vanilla.

Refrigerate, stirring or whisking every 7 to 10 minutes, until the mixture is cool but not thoroughly chilled and is beginning to thicken. Depending on the shape and size of the bowl and the depth of the mixture, this will take from 1 to 1¼ hours.

About 5 minutes before you anticipate that the coffee mixture will be properly chilled,

prepare the egg whites and whipped cream (a hand-held electric mixer will be useful for beating both). Beat the egg whites in a medium bowl until soft peaks form. Add the remaining ¼ cup sugar and continue beating until the whites stand in stiff peaks. Whip the cream in a separate medium bowl until it too stands in soft peaks. You may use the same beaters, and it is not necessary to wash them.

Scoop the whipped cream and egg whites onto the coffee mixture and, using a rubber spatula or a large wooden spoon, fold everything together quickly yet gently, until evenly blended and there are no drifts of unblended white. Pour the mixture into the prepared crust, mounding it in the center. Swirl the surface with a spoon to make a decorative pattern. Chill for several hours before serving.

Makes one 9-inch pie

If you want the fluff of a chiffon pie without the richness and calories from cream, this unorthodox version, lightened solely with beaten egg whites, will fit the bill. Unlike a traditional chiffon pie, this is baked, like a souffle, and has a texture that is light but not dry, yet more compact than a gelatin-based pie. In addition to pumpkin, cooked and mashed sweet potatoes, yams, and winter squash may be used with success in the filling.

pumpkin soufflé pie

Basic All-American Pie Dough for a 9-inch pie shell (page 20)

1½ cups cooked, mashed pumpkin or unsweetened canned pumpkin

⅔ cup brown sugar

4 egg yolks

1 teaspoon ground cinnamon

1 teaspoon ground ginger

½ teaspoon ground nutmeg

¼ teaspoon salt

¾ cup or more milk or evaporated milk

4 egg whites

¼ cup sugar

Preheat the oven to 425°F. Roll out the dough and fit it into a 9-inch pie pan. Trim and flute the edges (see page 22). Set aside.

Combine the pumpkin, brown sugar, egg yolks, cinnamon, ginger, nutmeg, and salt in a large bowl and whisk until smooth and evenly blended. Gently whisk in ¾ cup milk. The mixture should have the consistency of cooked hot cereal, such as oatmeal. If necessary, whisk in another ¼ cup or so of milk to achieve the right texture. Set aside.

Put the egg whites in a medium bowl and, using a hand-held electric beater or rotary beater, beat until soft peaks form. Add the sugar gradually, continuing to beat until the whites stand in peaks that droop just slightly when the beater is lifted. Stir or whisk a heaping spoonful of the whites into the pumpkin mixture, then scoop the remaining whites on top and, using a rubber spatula or large wooden spoon, fold together rapidly until you see no drifts of unblended white. Pour the mixture into the pie shell.

Bake for about 18 minutes, then reduce the heat to 300°F and bake for 50 to 55 minutes longer, until the filling has puffed dramatically and a knife inserted slightly off-center comes out almost clean, with no raw filling attached. Turn the oven off, set its door ajar, and let the pie cool for 20 minutes; the filling will sink as it cools. Serve the pie slightly warm or at room temperature, and refrigerate any leftovers.

Makes one 9-inch pie

candy (special/celebration) pies

With fresh fruit available (though not always good tasting) throughout the year, it is easy to forget that some pies can be made with simple ingredients independent of locality, season or availability. Some of these recipes, like the Sugar Cream (Hoosier) Pie, and Shoofly Pie, are quite venerable and have ancestors in ancient recipe books. Today they are nearly forgotten. Others, like Fudge Brownie Pie, and Peanut Butter Fudge Pie, are candylike confections. Mud Pie takes its name from its intense chocolate dessert. Regardless of their provenance, all of the recipes are sweet and satisfying, and they are geranteed to win a place in almost any dinner.

This pie isn't particularly delicate,
but it delivers a hefty shot of chocolate and peanut butter. Make it for pure enjoyment
and indulgence. Once the crust is done, the rest of it goes together in a flash.

peanut butter fudge pie

Crumb Crust for a 9-inch pie shell, made with chocolate wafer cookies (page 32)

12 ounces (1½ cups) cream cheese, at room temperature

1 cup smooth peanut butter

1 cup confectioners' sugar

⅓ cup unsweetened cocoa powder

1 can (14 ounces) sweetened condensed milk

1 teaspoon vanilla extract

¾ cup heavy (whipping) cream

Form and bake the crumb crust as directed in the recipe. Cool completely before filling.

Put the cream cheese and peanut butter in a large bowl and beat vigorously, using a hand-held electric mixer or a big wooden spoon, until blended and smooth. Combine and stir together the confectioners' sugar and cocoa powder, then sift them together, or shake them through a strainer, over the cream cheese mixture. Beat vigorously until smooth and evenly mixed. Beat in the sweetened condensed milk and vanilla.

Pour the cream into a medium bowl and whip with an electric mixer or rotary beater until it stands in soft peaks. Scoop the cream on top of the peanut butter mixture and, using a rubber spatula or a big wooden spoon, fold in the cream just until you see no drifts of unblended cream. Scoop the filling into the prepared crust, mounding it in the center, then make decorative swirls with the back of a spoon. Refrigerate for 4 to 6 hours or overnight before serving.

Makes one 9-inch pie

Dense and dark chocolate pies such as this are often called mud pies, a name that doesn't have too much appeal for me. If you want to be different and bake a pie rather than a cake for a birthday, this is the one to choose. The filling is solid enough to support all the candles you can stick into it, and it won't melt under the heat. A stand-type electric mixer is almost essential for beating the egg whites.

fudge brownie pie

Crumb Crust for a 9-inch pie shell, made with chocolate wafer cookies (page 32)

⅓ cup all-purpose flour

¼ teaspoon baking powder

¼ teaspoon salt

2 ounces (2 squares) unsweetened chocolate, broken into pieces or coarsely chopped

3 tablespoons unsalted butter

2 cups (12 ounces) semisweet chocolate morsels

3 eggs, at room temperature

⅔ cup sugar

1 tablespoon instant coffee granules

2 teaspoons vanilla extract

Form and bake the crumb crust as directed in the recipe, baking it for 8 minutes. Cool completely before filling.

Combine the flour, baking powder, and salt and sift them together onto a sheet of waxed paper. Set aside.

Place the unsweetened chocolate, butter, and 1 cup of the chocolate morsels in a medium-size, heavy-bottomed saucepan. Set over medium-low heat and cook, stirring frequently, for 5 to 7 minutes, or until the mixture is melted and smooth. While the chocolate melts, start beating the eggs.

Combine the eggs, sugar, instant coffee, and vanilla in a large bowl and beat with an electric mixer at high speed until the mixture is thick and foamy and about 4 times its original volume. (This will take 7 to 8 minutes using a stand-type electric mixer,

longer if you are using a hand-held electric mixer.) If you are using a stand-type mixer, remove the bowl from the stand when you're finished beating.

Add the warm chocolate mixture to the egg mixture and, with a rubber spatula or large wooden spoon, stir until the batter is streaked with chocolate. Sprinkle the flour mixture over the egg mixture and continue to stir taking care to reach the bottom of the bowl—until the batter is evenly mixed, with no unblended streaks. Stir in the remaining 1 cup chocolate morsels.

Pour the mixture into the prepared crust and bake for 25 to 30 minutes, until the filling has become slightly firm and has puffed slightly, and you see small cracks in a few places. Cool completely before serving.

Makes one 9-inch pie

Take a glance at any historical American cookbook, or anybody's old recipe file, and you are apt to find a version of shoofly pie. Though each varies slightly in its ingredients, the results, I have found, are quite similar, with a sweet, crisp topping covering a caramel-like filling. Like many simple recipes, the result is better than the sum of the parts, and the ingredients are so basic you might not even have to go to the store. In the Pennsylvania Dutch region, homemade shoofly pies can be purchased from the kitchen of almost every farmhouse.

shoofly pie

Basic All-American Pie Dough for a 9-inch pie shell (page 20)

TOPPING

1 cup all-purpose flour

½ cup brown sugar

½ teaspoon ground cinnamon

¼ teaspoon salt

½ cup vegetable shortening

FILLING

1 cup boiling water

1 teaspoon baking soda

1 cup dark corn syrup

Preheat the oven to 425°F. Roll out the dough and fit it into a 9-inch pie pan, then trim and flute the edges (see page 22). Set aside.

To make the topping, combine the flour, brown sugar, cinnamon, and salt in a large bowl. Stir together with a fork or whisk, making sure to break up any large lumps of brown sugar. Drop in the shortening and, using your fingertips or a pastry blender, blend the shortening into the dry ingredients until the mixture looks like small, irregular crumbs. Set aside.

To make the filling, in a small bowl stir together the boiling water and baking soda. Add the corn syrup and stir until evenly blended. Pour into the prepared pie shell. Sprinkle the crumb mixture over the top, distributing it as evenly as you can. Be careful not to spill the filling while carrying this pie to the oven, as it is very liquidy.

Bake for 10 minutes, then turn the heat down to 350°F and bake for 25 to 30 minutes more, until the topping is browned and the filling is set.

Serve warm or at room temperature.

Makes one 9-inch pie

In the oven this pie filling separates into two almost equal layers: a light, cakey top over a softly set caramel custard. Owing to its sweetness and richness, this pie is best served in small wedges, topped with unsweetened whipped cream.

caramel pie

Basic All-American Pie Dough for a 9-inch pie shell (page 20)

1½ cups brown sugar

1½ tablespoons all-purpose flour

¼ teaspoon salt

2 egg yolks

2 tablespoons unsalted butter, melted

¼ cup light or dark corn syrup

⅔ cup milk, warmed slightly

1 teaspoon vanilla extract

2 egg whites

2 tablespoons sugar

Preheat the oven to 350°F. Roll out the dough and fit it into a 9-inch pie pan, then trim and flute the edges (see page 22). Set aside.

In a large bowl, combine the brown sugar, flour, and salt. Stir and toss together with a fork or whisk until evenly blended, pressing to break up any large lumps of sugar. Add the egg yolks, butter, corn syrup, milk, and vanilla, and whisk until completely mixed.

In a small bowl, using a hand-held beater or electric mixer, beat the egg whites until soft peaks form. Add the sugar and continue beating until the whites stand in stiff peaks that droop slightly when the beater is lifted. Scoop the beaten whites on top of the brown sugar mixture and, using a rubber spatula or wooden spoon, stir and fold them together until there are no drifts of unblended white. Pour into the prepared pie shell.

Bake for about 45 minutes, or until the filling has puffed and browned and a knife inserted slightly off-center comes out almost clean, with just a few traces of wet—but not raw—custard on it.

Serve warm or at room temperature.

Makes one 9-inch pie

Fresh fruit in season is almost always better than canned, frozen, or preserved fruit. But this amazing and time-honored pie, a tribute to the dawn of the frozen fruit industry and the electric mixer, is best made the original way. In fact, the elbow grease required to whip this filling by hand is too daunting to think about; I wouldn't try it without a stand-type electric mixer. You will be impressed by the lofty volume and the good berry flavor achieved by so few ingredients—and a little electricity.

mile high strawberry pie

Basic All-American Pie Dough for a 9-inch pie shell (page 20)

4 egg whites

Pinch of salt

²/₃ cup sugar

1¼ cups (10 ounces) sliced, sweetened frozen strawberries, thawed and not drained

2 tablespoons fresh lemon juice

1 cup heavy (whipping) cream

Preheat the oven to 425°F. Roll out the pie dough and fit it into a 9-inch pie pan. Trim and flute the edges, then bake the pie shell fully, following the instructions on page 22. Cool completely before filling.

Put the egg whites and salt in the large bowl of an electric mixer and beat at moderate speed until they stand in soft, foamy peaks. Keep beating as you add the sugar in a steady stream, and continue to beat until the whites stand in stiff, firm peaks. Add the strawberries (along with any accumulated juices) and lemon juice, and beat at high speed for about 2 minutes, or until the mixture is thick and fluffy and stands in billowy peaks that droop slightly when the beater is lifted.

In a deep, narrow bowl or quart-size measuring cup, whip the cream until it stands in soft peaks and is about the consistency of the strawberry mixture. Scoop the cream on top of the berry mixture and, using a rubber spatula or large wooden spoon, stir and fold together until you don't see any streaks of unblended cream. Pile the mixture into the prepared pie shell, mounding it in the center—it will be several inches high—and chill for several hours or overnight before serving. After about 24 hours, the filling will begin to deflate.

Makes one 9-inch pie

Sugar pie is sometimes known as milk pie, although with such basic ingredients it could also be called humble pie. With its blend of crust and cream, it indeed has a soothing quality that will remind you of milk toast. The coconut, though not traditional, blends well with the other flavors, but you may leave it out if you wish.

sugar pie

Basic All-American Pie dough for a 9-inch pie shell (page 20)

1¼ cups white sugar, or brown sugar if you wish a darker filling

½ cup all-purpose flour

½ teaspoon ground nutmeg

¼ teaspoon salt

½ cup shredded coconut

1¼ cups milk

¾ cup heavy (whipping) cream

2 tablespoons unsalted butter, cut into 10 or 12 small pieces

Preheat the oven to 350°F. Roll out the dough and fit it into a 9-inch glass pie pan, then trim and flute the edges (see page 22).

In a large bowl, combine the sugar, flour, nutmeg, and salt, then stir and toss them together with a fork. Pour the mixture into a large strainer and, using your fingers or the back of a spoon, push it through the strainer directly into the pie shell. Sprinkle with the coconut. Set aside.

In a small saucepan, warm the milk and cream together over moderate heat until quite hot to your finger—do not let it boil. Pour evenly over the sugar mixture in the pie shell. Scatter the butter over the cream.

Bake for 55 to 60 minutes, or until the filling is set around the edges and has golden spots on top; it will not brown evenly. Don't worry if the center seems a little runny; it will firm up as it cools.

Serve warm or at room temperature.

Makes one 9-inch pie

index

The exact equivalents in the following tables have been rounded for convenience.

table of equivalents

LIQUID/DRY MEASURES

U.S.	Metric
¼ teaspoon	1.25 milliliters
½ teaspoon	2.5 milliliters
1 teaspoon	5 milliliters
1 tablespoon (3 teaspoons)	15 milliliters
1 fluid ounce (2 tablespoons)	30 milliliters
¼ cup	60 milliliters
⅓ cup	80 milliliters
½ cup	120 milliliters
1 cup	240 milliliters
1 pint (2 cups)	480 milliliters
1 quart (4 cups, 32 ounces)	960 milliliters
1 gallon (4 quarts)	3.84 liters
1 ounce (by weight)	28 grams
1 pound	454 grams
2.2 pounds	1 kilogram

LENGTH

U.S.	Metric
⅛ inch	3 millimeters
¼ inch	6 millimeters
½ inch	12 millimeters
1 inch	2.5 centimeters

OVEN TEMPERATURE

Fahrenheit	Celsius	Gas
250°	120°	½
275°	140°	1
300°	150°	2
325°	160°	3
350°	180°	4
375°	190°	5
400°	200°	6
425°	220°	7
450°	230°	8
475°	240°	9
500°	260°	10